THE BIBLE IN A YEAR COMPANION

VOLUME II: DAYS 121–243

Fr. Mike Schmitz

Jeff Cavins

Kara Logan

ASCENSION

West Chester, PA

Excerpts from the English translation of the *Catechism of the Catholic Church* for use in the United States of America © 1994 United States Catholic Conference, Inc.–Libreria Editrice Vaticana. Used with permission. English translation of the *Catechism of the Catholic Church: Modifications from the Editio Typica* © 1997 United States Conference of Catholic Bishops–Libreria Editrice Vaticana.

Unless otherwise noted, Scripture passages are from the Revised Standard Version–Second Catholic Edition © 2006 by the Division of Christian Education of the National Council of the Churches of Christ in the United States of America. Used by permission. All rights reserved.

Ascension
PO Box 1990
West Chester, PA 19380
1-800-376-0520
ascensionpress.com

Cover design: Rosemary Strohm

Printed in the United States of America
22 23 24 25 26 5 4 3 2 1

ISBN 978-1-954881-15-0

Dedicated to the 2021 listeners of
The Bible in a Year (with Fr. Mike Schmitz)™
featuring Jeff Cavins.

Thank you for being the first group to journey through Scripture with us. Your ideas, questions, and feedback inspired this book.

We're praying for you—please pray for us, and we cannot wait to see you tomorrow.

CONTENTS

INTRODUCTION

Volume II! Wow. That means something ... it means you made it through Volume I. (Yes, I know. I'm pretty sharp!)

Seriously, though ... you are on your way. You might have been intimidated at the start of this journey through the Bible—particularly by reading all of these books of the Old Testament. Maybe you had some thoughts of self-doubt: *Can I really get through the entire Bible?* Maybe you had tried to read it before and stopped after a month. *How can I possibly read through the Bible in 365 days?*

But here you are.

And I think that one of the things we have learned is that we just have to keep putting one foot in front of the other. For many of us, there were some days when we were not able to listen. We may have even had a week when we "fell off the wagon," when we got off track. But at those times we were reminded that we are called to perseverance, not perfection.

Think of all of those people in the Bible that we heard about over the past hundred days or so. Abraham wasn't perfect, but he persevered and walked in faithfulness to the Lord until the day when he held God's promise in his arms. Jacob was a deceiver and ran away from home, but God directed his steps to reconciliation with his brother Esau. David was anointed early in his life and experienced a closeness with the Lord, but he sinned; he repented, though, and God drew David back to his heart.

Recall the chaos of the period of the judges. The people that God had made his own were living as strangers to him. Yet the Lord kept calling, and they kept walking.

Just like us.

We have been through a lot over these first hundred days or so. We have been challenged quite a bit. God has confronted us with his true character. God has revealed to us who he is. He has revealed a heart for those who are lost. In addition, we have seen the fickleness and failings of God's Chosen People—as well as our own.

And yet, just like the people of Israel, we keep walking. Our journey with the Lord continues. We have learned that perseverance is more important than perfection. So we keep putting one foot in front of the other.

–Fr. Mike Schmitz

HOW TO USE THIS
BIBLE IN A *YEAR* COMPANION

This *Companion* provides a number of ways to help you remember God's Word and live your life through the lens of Scripture. In Volume II you will be guided through days 121–243 of the podcast by three features: **Reflect on the Word**, **Take It to Prayer**, and **Dive Deeper**.

- In **Reflect on the Word**, you will see a summary of Fr. Mike's commentary on the readings for that day. These are important things to remember and key takeaways to help you go deeper into the Story.

- In **Take It to Prayer**, you will pray along with Fr. Mike every day, using a word-for-word transcript of the prayer he prays in the podcast. Read it aloud as you listen, repeat it throughout the day, or pray it before you go to sleep.

- Every day, you will be given an opportunity to **Dive Deeper** into the Scriptures. Sometimes, this section will include an *image* of a key element or event mentioned in the Bible or an *answer* to a frequently asked question about the readings. Some days, it might be a *prayer prompt* to use during your prayer time or a *challenge* to live out what you have heard in your life.

In addition, a **time period introduction** by Jeff Cavins is included at the start of every period of salvation history. Here, Jeff explains the significance of the period's color, its key events and figures, and any significant changes in the lead-up to that time. At the end of each period, Jeff offers a **time period review**, a short recap of what happened and review questions to help you recognize how much you learned.

Reflect on the **Word**

- This genealogy in Chronicles tells the story from Abraham to David. Then the family line will go on from David to Jesus, who had been promised from the very beginning.

- Some of the names may be unfamiliar, but each individual has a place in salvation history.

- David is now the king of Judah. He is going to battle Ish-bosheth.

- Asahel is chasing Abner, a military leader under Saul. Although Abner asks Asahel to stop chasing him, Asahel continues. So Abner has to kill him in self-defense. Abishai and Joab then chase Abner to avenge the death of their brother. Abner calls for an end to the cycle of violence.

- Violence does not simply end on its own; it must be ended by those who are fighting.

- Jesus allows violence to fall upon himself, suffering for the sake of the unrighteous. This puts an end to the cycle in many ways.

- Jesus gives us an opportunity to be part of the cycle of mercy—the cycle of allowing oneself to suffer for another. He calls us to forgive. Forgiveness, though, is one of the most difficult teachings of Christianity.

- We must ask ourselves if we are angry or desire revenge—and how we can let go of animosity toward others and forgive.

Take It to **Prayer**

Father in heaven, we give you praise and glory today. We thank you so much for the unfolding of time. We thank you for the unfolding of the story of salvation and the story of how, Lord God, you are willing to take time. You are willing to be patient, not only with us in our weakness and our littleness and our falseness—you are also willing to be patient with the passage of time, with other people's decisions, and the fact that we have to grow and it takes time to grow. And so we thank you. We thank you for being patient with us. We thank you for giving us time. We thank you for allowing this time to be used. So we ask you, help us to use this time to grow. Help us to use this time not as wasted time, not as stalling-out time, but as time where we can always find you. And you will always, always find us where we are in this moment. We give you praise, and we thank you. We make this prayer in the name of Jesus Christ, our Lord. Amen.

Dive **Deeper**

Today in prayer, consider if you are angry or desire revenge. Ask God to help you recognize how you can let go of animosity toward others and forgive, and pray for help.

Reflect on the **Word**

- God's Word is rooted in history. We will follow the story through the line of David.

- Abner wants to reconcile with David, but violence begets violence.

- When Joab learns that Abner is near, he kills Abner in revenge for the death of his brother Asahel, though Abner killed him in self-defense.

- David publicly mourns the death of Abner, his enemy. He even instructs Joab to wear sackcloth and tear his garments in grief.

- Because of his character, David is a good and wise leader.

- We are called to forgive our enemies.

- We need wisdom in our relationships with people who have hurt us and others.

- We can grow in trust and pray that the cycle of violence ends in our hearts so that we can forgive and be reconciled.

Take It to **Prayer**

Father in heaven, we give you praise, and we thank you. We thank you for the difficulty of these days. Honestly, God, it is difficult to get through these names. And we just have to admit that yes, they mean something. Yes, they are powerful. They are meaningful. And they are difficult. That is worth noting. It is worth noting that. Lord, thank you. Thank you for your Word that is rooted in history and rooted in reality, rooted in people's actual stories so that all of these names are markers. All of these names are persons. All of these names are untold stories. So many of these names we have here, Lord, are names of people that we don't know much about other than their name and other than the fact that they were critical to you. They were loved by you. They were known by you. And they were part of your story to redeem the world. So in the difficulty, Lord, we ask that you please give us strength and give us patience so that we can hear the words we need to hear and we can become the people you want us to become. In Jesus' name we pray. Amen.

Dive **Deeper**

Spend some time today reflecting on your relationships with those who have hurt you. Can you be reconciled with them and even become friends? If a relationship is not possible, allow God to enter into your heart and give you the grace to forgive them.

Reflect on the **Word**

- In 2 Samuel 4, David seeks to establish a kingdom of justice.

- He seeks to have mercy on his enemy Ish-bosheth, who has been hailed as the new king.

- When Ish-bosheth is murdered by Rechab and Baanah, David does not reward the two men but condemns their evil act. He has them executed in the name of justice.

- Under David, Israel will be a united kingdom under the Law of the Lord.

- In 1 Chronicles, David is shown to prefigure the Messiah.

- It is believed that 1 Chronicles was written after the Exile, reflecting how much the people of Israel have suffered. The people long for the reestablishment of the kingdom and Temple worship.

- The eternal God works in time and history, continuing to guide and protect his people out of love.

Take It to **Prayer**

Father in heaven, we give you praise and glory. We thank you so much for your Word. We thank you for just the fact that you have worked in history, and you continue to work in history. Lord God, you have worked with every one of these people and every one of these families and tribes, just like you work with us, every one of us listening to your Word being proclaimed. All of our families, strong and weak. All of our families, whole and broken. All of our families, united and divided. Lord God, you are part of history. You are the God of history. You are the God of eternity. You are the God of our history, and you lead us and call us into eternity. And so we give you thanks, and we give you praise. Please receive our praise today—on this day 123 of listening to your Word, of being shaped by your Word. We thank you and praise you. In Jesus' name we pray. Amen.

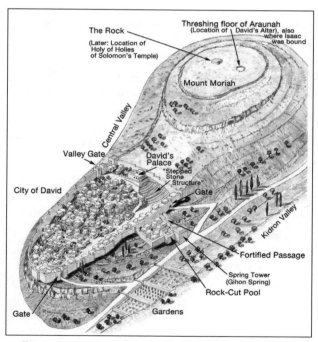

Illustration and caption from Ritmeyer Archaeological Design

Dive **Deeper**

JERUSALEM AT THE TIME OF DAVID

This is a reconstruction drawing of the City of David on the eastern hill of Jerusalem. King David captured the stronghold from the Jebusites. (See 2 Samuel 5:6-7 in tomorrow's readings.)

Reflect on the **Word**

- David was anointed king by Samuel at a young age. After years of fighting in Saul's army, as a leader of warriors, and as the leader of Judah, he is now thirty and king of a united Israel.

- When David becomes the king of Israel, he makes Jerusalem its capital, choosing it as his stronghold.

- Hiram, the king of Tyre, seeks to build a palace for David. Here, one king recognizes the power and greatness of another.

- The Philistines, when they learn that David has become king of Israel, want to fight him. David does what he has consistently done—he seeks the will of the Lord. After the first battle, David again seeks the counsel of the Lord and is told to attack the Philistines at the rear.

- In our lives, we should pray for God's guidance whether we should fight a certain battle or not.

- In Deuteronomy 17:17, the Law says that a king should not have multiple wives "lest his heart turn away." In disobedience to this command of the Lord, David takes many wives and concubines (see 2 Samuel 5:13).

- As a result, the majority of David's problems will come not from external enemies but from his own family.

- Just like David, all of us are a mix of greatness and brokenness. We must continually ask the Lord where he wants us to help, serve, fight, and repent. As Christians, we have the strength of the indwelling Spirit we receive at Baptism to help us.

Take It to **Prayer**

Father in heaven, we give you praise. We thank you, and we give you honor and glory. Lord God, thank you. Thank you for your Word. Thank you for letting us see in chapters one through eight of the book of Chronicles the ways in which you have unfolded this family. You have gone back in and helped us review, Lord God. You have helped us review the lives of your family, the lives of the Jewish people. Those fathers and sons, those sisters and daughters, those people that you have called out of nothingness to be yours, to be a people peculiarly your own. Lord God, we ask you please to help us to be yours as well. Because you have called us from obscurity. Lord God, you have called us from nothingness into being. You have called us from being into being your children. We are so grateful for you, Lord God. Please receive our praise. Receive our thanks. Please be with us this day. In Jesus' name we pray. Amen.

Dive **Deeper**

Illustration and caption from Ritmeyer Archaeological Design

DAVID'S PALACE IN JERUSALEM

This reconstruction drawing shows the palace of King David. (See 2 Samuel 5:9-11.) In the excavations of 1978–1985, a stepped stone structure was discovered that may have served as a foundation for David's palace higher up the hill.

Reflect on the **Word**

- The first half of Psalm 89 praises God for his faithfulness, goodness, and strength in defeating the enemy. The second half of this psalm speaks of loss, defeat, and disgrace. At the end, the psalmist says, "Blessed be the LORD for ever" (Psalm 89:52)—he praises the Lord in all these things.

- In 2 Samuel 6, David wants to bring the Ark of the Covenant back to Jerusalem.

- Recall that the Ark contains the Ten Commandments, Aaron's staff, and manna.

- The Ark is being brought to Jerusalem on a cart drawn by oxen. When the oxen stumble, Uzzah reaches out to steady the Ark with his hand—and he is slain by the Lord for this act of irreverence. While this seems unjust, we need to recall the Law. The Ark can only be transported by the priests, and they are not allowed to touch it (see Numbers 4:15). When Uzzah touches it, the reverence that the holiest object in existence deserves is not observed.

- The price of unrepented sin is eternal life. When we choose sin, we are saying, "God, I know what you want, but I want to do what I want." Ultimately, unrepented sin leads to spiritual death.

- Mary, the Mother of God, is the "new Ark of the Covenant," who carries the Word made flesh and "the living bread which came down from heaven" (John 6:51) in her womb.

- Just as David leaps and dances with joy before the Ark, the infant in Elizabeth's womb (St. John the Baptist) leaps for joy in the presence of Mary, the new Ark. Here we see how Jesus fulfills all the promises and foreshadowing of the Old Testament.

Take It to **Prayer**

Father in heaven, we give you praise and glory. We thank you for hearing this prayer of David, this prayer of a heart that has been lifted up and a heart that has been thrown down. A heart that has been exultant in joy and a heart that has been broken in sorrow. A heart that has been triumphant in victory, and a heart that has been devastated in defeat. And this is our hearts too, Lord. We come before you however our day is going, however our week is going, however the season of our life is going right now. We come before you in victory and in defeat. We come before you in joy, and we come before you in grief. Because your love encompasses all things. Joy and grief. Victory and defeat. Weakness and strength. And so we come before you because you are a good, good dad. Please receive us into your heart. Receive us into your embrace this day. In Jesus' name we pray. Amen.

Dive **Deeper**

Today, make Psalm 89:52 your prayer: "Blessed be the Lord for ever." Ask for the grace to praise the Lord in times of joy and in times of grief.

Reflect on the **Word**

- At first, the twelve tribes of Israel were a loose federation.

- In 2 Samuel 8, we see that David works to bring the twelve tribes together in a united kingdom. He seeks to accomplish this by conquering the nations around them.

- There is a reason the stories of Saul and David are repeated in Chronicles: their author, Ezra, writes of the past to give the people a vision for the future—with a king and Temple worship.

- Ezra seeks to give Israel a clear sense of God's presence, both in the past and the present.

- He reminds them of their pedigree, of where they came from. He writes not only about David but of the other mighty men of the time.

- One of these men is Uriah the Hittite, the husband of Bathsheba, with whom David will commit adultery. David will arrange for Uriah to die in battle.

- The events described in the Bible are not incidental or arbitrary. They are meant for our direction, our education, and our vision.

Take It to **Prayer**

Father in heaven, we give you praise, and we do know that with you we can do valiantly. Without you we can do nothing. If we remain in you, then all things are possible. If we remain in you, then we can bear fruit, fruit that will last. And yet if we remove ourselves from you, if we remove ourselves from your presence and from your power and from your help and from your holiness, then there is nothing that we can do. We can bear no fruit, and we can make no difference in our lives. So we need you, God, not only for our existence, but also for perseverance. We need you not only for fruitfulness but also for faithfulness. So please, Lord God, help us to be faithful and fruitful. Help us to persevere and to be yours forever. In Jesus' name we pray. Amen.

Dive **Deeper**

By recounting their past, Ezra reminds the Israelites of God's presence then and in the present. In your prayer today, recall a significant moment in your relationship with God that reminded you of his presence. Thank the Lord for his presence in your life.

Reflect on the **Word**

- In 2 Samuel 9, David has asked to build a temple for God, but his successor will do this. So David wants to know what he can do for the Lord.

- He also wants to honor the covenant he made with Jonathan.

- Jonathan's remaining son is Mephibosheth. As Saul's grandson, he would be David's enemy, but David treats him like his own son.

- Typically, a new king would have any descendants of the old king killed. Instead, David shows compassion and wisdom by honoring Mephibosheth.

- How can we show kindness for the Lord's sake in our own lives?

- David's men are characterized by bravery, valor, and wisdom. They are dedicated and persevering in defending the king and fighting against Israel's enemies.

Take It to **Prayer**

Father in heaven, we give you praise and thank you so much. Lord God, we thank you for this day. We thank you for this season of our lives. We thank you for guiding us and speaking to us for the last 127 days and shaping our eyes, our hearts, our minds by your Word and by who you truly are, who you are calling us to be. We ask that you please fill us with the spirit of courage. Fill us with a singleness of purpose. Fill us with the wisdom to be able to know which actions to take and to know which actions to refrain from taking. We make this prayer in the name of Jesus Christ, our Lord. Amen.

Dive **Deeper**

Apart from the Bible, *is there any evidence for the existence of David?*

Modern archaeology continues to uncover the past and corroborate much of the biblical narrative, so we should never discount the history described in the Bible due to a lack of current archaeological evidence.

In 1993, an excavation at Tel Dan in Israel led by archaeologist Avraham Biran discovered an inscription that corroborates Scripture's record.

The inscription *bet David* ("house of David") was found on a stone slab (or *stele*) dating to the ninth century BC that memorializes an Aramean king's defeat of an Israelite king and the "king of the House of David." This *stele* affirms that Israel and Judah were divided. In addition, archaeologists digging in Jerusalem just south of the Temple mount have found a seal with a biblical name from the house of Judah.[*]

–Jeff Cavins

---

[*] See "The Tel Dan Inscription: The First Historical Evidence of King David from the Bible," *Bible History Daily* (blog), Biblical Archaeology Society, June 11, 2021, biblicalarchaeology.org, and "Impression of King Hezekiah's Royal Seal Discovered in Excavations in Jerusalem," ScienceDaily, December 2, 2015, sciencedaily.com.

Reflect on the **Word**

- We continue to witness David's goodness and kindness. When the king of the Ammonites dies, David sends ambassadors to offer his condolences to the deceased king's son.

- To humiliate the ambassadors of Israel, the new king of the Ammonites, Hanun, shaves off half their beards and cuts their garments at the middle. Since this would have caused them shame and disgrace, in kindness David lets them remain in Jericho until their beards grow back fully.

- Joab tells the soldiers, "Be of good courage … for our people, and for the cities of our God; and may the Lord do what seems good to him" (2 Samuel 10:12). Unsurprisingly, they win the battle.

- In 1 Chronicles 13, we see the familiar story of David wanting to bring the Ark of the Covenant to Jerusalem.

- We too are called to live in God's presence.

- God is present in the Eucharist, the other sacraments, and the Bible in a special way. But he is also present wherever we are. Whenever we call upon his name, we become aware of his presence.

2 Samuel 10, 1 Chronicles 13, Psalm 31

Take It to **Prayer**

*Father in heaven, we give you praise, and we thank you. We are reminded by your
Word today to love you. As David said, "Love the LORD, all you his saints!" To love you,
God, is our highest good. It's our highest duty. It's our highest call. It's our highest
honor, to be able not only to be loved by you, but to love you in return—which makes
no sense whatsoever, God, that you would even care. Why would you even care that
we love you? And yet, it matters. And yet, our tokens of affection, even our small
gestures of love, our small gestures of faithfulness, our gestures of worship, even this
podcast, Lord, allowing us to hear your Word—you receive that. You receive that as
a gift of love to you, and we think, "Lord, you're the one who is loving us by speaking
your word into our minds and our hearts and to our ears and to our lives." And yet, you
see this, and you receive it as our act of love to you, our act of thanksgiving, our act of
worship to you to simply allow you to speak to us. So Lord, we just want to give you
love in return for the love you have given us. So please, help us to love you this day.
"Love the LORD, all you his saints! ... Be strong, and let your heart take courage,
all you who wait for the LORD!" In Jesus' name we pray. Amen.*

Dive **Deeper**

Since Jesus is truly present in the Holy Eucharist—Body, Blood,
Soul, and Divinity—set a time this week to go to Adoration.

Reflect on the **Word**

- In 2 Samuel 11, we read that David sends Joab and his army into battle while he remains in Jerusalem. In the ancient world, a king typically led his soldiers in battle; he literally fought for his people. In previous battles, David did this, but now he is sending someone else to lead.

- Sin usually begins small, by neglecting our daily duties and avoiding the everyday tasks God has given us.

- David sees Bathsheba, the wife of Uriah the Hittite, one of the trusted men who has risked his life for the people of Israel. David sends for Bathsheba and commits adultery with her, and she becomes pregnant.

- Though David sends for Uriah to go home, Uriah refuses as he wants to continue fighting for Israel. So David conspires to have him die in battle, this man who has been laying his life on the line for him and the people of Israel.

- This grave sin of David began simply by his seeking comfort rather than doing his duty as king.

- God convicts David of the evil he has done, and he repents. Psalm 32, like Psalm 51, is a prayer of repentance.

- Even the worst sin does not mean the end. God knows David's heart, and he keeps calling David back to him. He continues calling us back as well when we sin.

- What should we do when we have sinned? We must seek God's forgiveness and mercy.

Take It to **Prayer**

Father in heaven, we give you praise and thank you. Thank you for this Psalm 32. Thank you for the fact that even in our sin we can call upon you, and you hear our voice. You hear our prayers. Lord, in our imperfection, you meet us with your mercy. In our sins, you meet us with your grace. And so we are so grateful. We are so grateful because we in so many ways are like David. And we in so many ways turn away from what we know you are calling us to do and who we know you are calling us to be. And so we ask you, please, renew your mercy in us. As your mercies are renewed each morning, renew them in us—because we need you, and we need your mercy. We thank you and give you praise. In Jesus' name we pray. Amen.

Dive **Deeper**

Illustration and caption from Ritmeyer Archaeological Design

RABBAH

These are the fortification walls of Rabbah (modern Amman Citadel), parts of which date from the time of David. (See 2 Samuel 11:1.)

Reflect on the **Word**

- David is a flawed hero. He is a sinner and broken man.

- David's sin in the dark needs to be brought into the light for God to save him. He is an example of God's ability to save.

- For all of us, God sometimes needs to "uncover" our sins, bringing into the light what we have done in the dark. He does this because he loves us and wants us to turn back to him.

- Nathan the prophet tells David that the Lord forgives him but that there are consequences to his actions.

- In 1 Chronicles 16, we read that David establishes the Ark in a tent. Again, the focus is on the kingdom and worship.

- Ultimately, God wants his kingdom to be established throughout the world—which will occur with the coming of the Messiah, Jesus.

- As we have seen, God wants his people to worship him in a particular way. David appoints certain Levites to be ministers before the Ark of the Lord "to invoke, to thank, and to praise the LORD, the God of Israel" (1 Chronicles 16:4). This is a good model for our prayer life.

- In Psalm 51, David reveals a fourth element of prayer—repentance. Repentance involves turning away from evil, living in the light, and seeking the Lord.

Take It to **Prayer**

Father in heaven, we give you praise, and we thank you. We thank you for calling us to repent. We thank you for reminding us of our sin. Thank you for reminding us of our sin and our need for mercy. And also thank you for offering your gift of mercy. Lord God, we find ourselves so often sliding like David did yesterday, in yesterday's reading: Sliding away from where you are calling us on mission, to live off mission. Sliding from where you anointed us to be, from belonging to you to rejecting you.

And we find ourselves so often as David does today, where Nathan said, "You thought this was done in the dark. But the Lord God is going to bring this into the light." And Lord God, to save us, you often reveal our wounds. To save us, you often reveal our sins. To save us, you often bring what needs to be brought into the light. And so, God, we say yes to that. We say, "OK, go ahead, Lord. Whatever you need to do in my life so that I may not be lost. Whatever you need to do in my life so that I can be yours again. You have my permission. So be it. Amen." Help us to say this, Lord God. In Jesus' name we pray. Amen.

Dive **Deeper**

Sin needs to be brought to the light so we can receive
God's forgiveness. We see this in the example of David.
Today, resolve to bring anything done in darkness to
the light and to turn back to God.

Reflect on the **Word**

- David wants to build a house for the Lord. But the Lord says he will build David a house.

- As we have seen, God told the prophet Samuel to anoint David as king of his people Israel because he was a man after the Lord's heart. God does not care about outward appearances; he looks into the heart.

- In 1 Chronicles 17, God reaffirms that David's dynasty will endure forever— that through his descendants, there will be a kingdom that blesses the entire world.

- David repents of sins, but he must live with their consequences.

- In 2 Samuel 13, we read how David's son Amnon lusts after Tamar, his half sister. He takes her, though she protests, arguing for her dignity as a human being. By doing this, Amnon destroys Tamar's future.

- Many today, like Tamar, feel they are used up and cannot be loved. In Jesus, we have hope because our God takes our brokenness and makes us whole.

- Ultimately, Absalom avenges his sister by killing his half brother Amnon. This begins Absalom's rebellion against his father David.

- When David learns that Amnon raped Tamar, he is angry but does nothing. He does not defend his daughter or confront his son. He does not act like a father. This failure will mark David's life with his family. His actions do not live up to his high calling.

Take It to **Prayer**

Father in heaven, we give you praise. We thank you because we do find ourselves in battles. We find ourselves called upon to act, called upon to speak, called upon to refrain from acting, and called upon to be silent. All these different times, Lord, it's so confusing sometimes how we should act and how we should not act—when we should move and when we should not move. Lord, especially when you have entrusted your children to our care, it is hard to know when discipline is called for and when mercy is called for. It's hard to know when justice is called for and when forgiveness and clemency is called for. And so, God, we just ask for your wisdom in making decisions, your wisdom in assisting others, your wisdom in serving others, and your wisdom in leading others. Because, God, it is often complex. Life is often complex. And the next step is not always absolutely clear. And so we pray for wisdom to know what to do, to know how to move forward, to know how to be yours, and to know how to actually help the people around us. Help us to be the kind of people who can help the people around us. We make this prayer in the name of Jesus Christ, our Lord. Amen.

Dive **Deeper**

How could God *permit Tamar to be assaulted?*

God permits evil to bring about an even greater good. But it is difficult to see the goodness that comes from horrible situations like the assault of Tamar.

Yet we can learn from Tamar's story. David's sin of lust leads to lust within his family, and lust leads Amnon to hatred.

Here, we see how sin can bear terrible fruit within a family and even destroy it. Yet, in the New Covenant, there is hope of healing for those who have had evil done to them. We do not see Tamar's healing in the Old Testament, but we know that Jesus brings healing and hope for those who have been abused.

–Kara Logan

Reflect on the **Word**

- Joab, leader of the army, hires a woman to tell David a parable that convinces him to allow his estranged son Absalom to return.

- Joab is loyal to David. It is likely that he sees Absalom as a threat to David if he remains in exile, where he can raise a revolt.

- Absalom shows no sign of repentance for killing his brother.

- David does not really forgive Absalom. While he permits Absalom to return to Jerusalem, he does not allow him into his presence for two years.

- God is not like this with us. He calls us to repentance—to turn away from our sins and return to him. If we repent, he fully forgives us and restores our relationship with him.

- In 2 Samuel 15, we will see that true forgiveness requires true repentance. Without forgiveness and reconciliation, there is rebellion.

- We need to come before the Lord and let go of whatever we have chosen over him.

- In Jesus, we have true forgiveness and full access to the Father's house and heart.

2 Samuel 14, 1 Chronicles 18, Psalm 14

Take It to **Prayer**

Father in heaven, we give you thanks, and we give you praise. You are a good God, and you are a good dad. Lord God, you are a good dad. You are a good Father, and you continue to meet us. You forgive us completely. But you also call us to complete repentance. You offer forgiveness totally, but you also call us to totally come back to you. And so help us, please, Father. Help us do that. Help us to come back totally so that your mercy may totally transform us. That your grace may totally transform us. That your love may totally renew us. Lord God, bring us back to you. Let your face shine on us, and we shall be saved. In Jesus' name we pray. Amen.

Dive **Deeper**

True repentance means being truly sorry for our sins and turning away from them—whatever this takes, regardless of how difficult this might be. If we approach God with repentance, he forgives us and restores us to "full access" to him. Pray the Act of Contrition and recommit yourself to the Lord.

Reflect on the **Word**

- Psalm 3 is a psalm of trust, written by David as he is fleeing from Absalom. David is saying that he will trust in the Lord in the midst of battle.

- When Absalom gathers the people at Hebron to fight against him, David knows that he has to flee.

- As David leads the people out of Jerusalem, he allows everyone to walk by him to ensure that they are all safe. Since the people are aware of his failures as a king and a father, David must endure his shame as they walk past him. There is a certain nobility in this act.

- In an act of trust, David commands the priests to return the Ark of the Covenant to Jerusalem. He knows that he will be in the Lord's presence again if he wills it.

- If we have not yet accepted someone's forgiveness, we have an opportunity to do so today.

- If there is someone we have forgiven, reach out to them and seek reconciliation.

- All of David's issues with Absalom started with his inaction. We need the Lord to help us do what we need to do, when we need to.

Take It to **Prayer**

*Father in heaven, we praise you, and we give you thanks. Lord, we do thank you.
We offer this word of trust, this word of confidence in you and your goodness and
your faithfulness—even in times of insecurity, even in times of uncertainty, even
in times of great trial and battle where the enemy is winning. We declare our
trust in you this day and every day in Jesus' name. Amen.*

Dive **Deeper**

Why did Absalom *hate his father, King David, so deeply?
Why couldn't David love and forgive him?*

We read in 2 Samuel 13:21 that David, after hearing what Amnon
did to Tamar, is "very angry." However, he does nothing to rectify the
situation, and Absalom refuses to forgive his father, David, for not
avenging the rape of his sister. David's absence and his permissive
parenting in turn leads Absalom to take matters into his own hands
and kill Amnon in revenge.

The Bible never mentions that David forgives Absalom, yet it does note
that "the king's heart went out to Absalom" (2 Samuel 14:1). While
David brings Absalom back, he does not call him into his presence for
two years. Absalom also makes no effort to repent and ask for David's
forgiveness. We soon learn that Absalom seeks to usurp David's throne.

In the end, it seems that Absalom never truly repents of killing his
brother. But David also never manifests the true forgiveness of a father.
In the events that follow his sin with Bathsheba, David is permissive
and lax with his children. His household is in chaos because there
is no real leadership and no true reconciliation. David's kingdom is
imperfect. Humanity awaits the new and everlasting kingdom of the
New Covenant, in the Church, where we receive grace and forgiveness.

–Kara Logan

Reflect on the **Word**

- In 2 Samuel 16, Ziba, the servant of Mephibosheth (the son of Jonathan), tells David that Mephibosheth will wait in Jerusalem to see who wins, David or Absalom. After they destroy one another, he will pick up the pieces.

- In 2 Samuel 19, though, we learn that Mephibosheth is not a traitor to David. We need to keep this in mind as we continue.

- Shime-i, of the house of Saul, curses David. Abishai, one of David's right-hand men, offers to cut off his head. David's response, though, reveals that he has indeed been humbled. He says that he is not so good and innocent that he does not deserve these curses.

- This is a great sign of repentance to say, "If you knew my heart and how much I have sinned against the Lord, you would know that your criticism of me doesn't cover half of it."

- David remembers his sins—and the prophecy that he would experience much disgrace in the sight of the people.

- In 1 Chronicles 21, we read that David wants to number the people of Israel. Joab advises against this, but David insists. By conducting a new census, David is implying that the people of Israel are not God's people anymore but his.

- In our readings today, we see what happens when we do not care what the Lord wants.

Take It to **Prayer**

Father in heaven, we give you praise and thank you. We honor you and give you glory, the glory you deserve. We give you the praise and honor and worship and thanksgiving of this day. Lord, as we follow the story of David, we ask that you please help us to discern in our own hearts where we need to be convicted of sin. Help us to see in our own hearts where we are called to be innocent, where we are called to be humbled, where we are called to be lifted up, where we are called to be strengthened, where we are called to receive encouragement, and where we are called to be open to criticism. Lord God, help us to be wise in the voices that we listen to and the voices that we pay attention to. And of all the voices that we hear in the course of the day, let yours be the one that is the loudest, that is the clearest, and is the one that goes directly to our hearts. In Jesus' name we pray. Amen.

Dive **Deeper**

***Why was it wrong** for David to conduct a census of the people?*

In the ancient world, a census was often undertaken to levy taxes. In other words, it was a way for a king to exert his authority over his subjects. The events recorded here in 1 Chronicles occurred just after David defeated the Philistines, raising his stock among the people. In his pride, David went against the wishes of God by seeking to make the Lord's people his own.

As a consequence, he had to choose one of three punishments (see 1 Chronicles 21:11-12). Here, David is an illustration of what the Bible says about a puffed-up spirit: "Pride goes before destruction, and a haughty spirit before a fall" (Proverbs 16:18).

–Jeff Cavins

Reflect on the **Word**

- In 2 Samuel 17, Ahithophel tells Absalom that he will lead twelve thousand men into battle just to kill David. The people will be spared, though, and brought back to Jerusalem.

- Hushai, the spy that David has sent to pose as Absalom's servant, encourages Absalom to lead the army instead.

- When Ahithophel learns that Absalom will lead the battle instead, he commits suicide.

- In 1 Chronicles 21, David decides to make the site of Ornan's threshing floor the place of the Temple.

- David begins collecting the materials needed for the Temple, but it is his son Solomon who will actually complete the work.

- In John 4, Jesus meets the Samaritan woman at the well, who says, "Our fathers worshiped on this mountain; and you say that in Jerusalem is the place where men ought to worship" (John 4:20). But Jesus replies, "The hour is coming, and now is, when the true worshipers will worship the Father in spirit and truth" (John 4:23).

- Here, we see a foreshadowing of the Holy Eucharist, given by Jesus at the Last Supper and celebrated in every place throughout the world during Mass.

- In Baptism, we became temples of the Holy Spirit. We need to live as worthy temples of the Lord.

Take It to **Prayer**

Father in heaven, we give you thanks. We praise your name, and we give you glory. We thank you for your justice because your justice is that you are right and you are true and you are fair. What we deserve you are willing to give. But we also thank you, Lord God, for your mercy. And we know that in your mercy you do not contradict justice, but in your mercy you fulfill justice—in yourself and in giving your Son as the sacrifice for my sin, as a sacrifice for our sins. You show yourself to be a God of justice and mercy in your one heart as you are one God and you are one character—truly consistent, just, and merciful. And so we thank you. I thank you, God, for your justice, that you are not fickle. I thank you for your mercy, that you are love. Please receive our thanks and praise this day in Jesus' name. Amen.

Dive **Deeper**

True worship—true faith—must cost something for it to be real. What does this mean to you? What has your faith cost you? Why is it worth the cost?

Reflect on the **Word**

- In 1 Chronicles 23, David establishes what Temple worship is to look like. He changes some of the former rules.

- Since the Temple is larger than the Tent of Meeting and is a permanent structure, there is a necessary shift in the type and amount of work that needs to be done. So David restructures the service of the Levites, reducing the minimum age for serving from thirty to twenty.

- In 2 Samuel 18, we read that Absalom is defeated and killed.

- Though Joab knows that David wants Absalom to live, he takes matters into his own hands and kills Absalom. Twenty thousand men have died in the battle with Absalom.

- When David hears of Absalom's death, he immediately begins mourning.

- Up until this point, David has not been a good father. He does not claim Absalom as his son until he hears of his death.

- God the Father claims Jesus as his Son—and he claims us as his sons and daughters through Baptism.

Take It to **Prayer**

Father in heaven, we praise you. We do. We take our refuge in you. We ask that you please number us. Count us among those who are righteous. Count us among those who trust in you and not in our own strength, but who seek to do your will in all things. Lord God, any way that we have taken ourselves away from your will in great ways and in small ways, we return to you with our whole heart and ask that you please not only lift us up, but help us to come back. Not only make us strong, but help us to return to you. We place ourselves in your hands. We surrender to your lordship, to you being God and Father forever. And we commit our hearts and our lives once again to you, in the name of your Son, Jesus. Amen.

Dive **Deeper**

David did not carry out his responsibilities as a father well. Is there a responsibility in your life that you have not fulfilled to the best of your abilities? If so, take some time today to ask God's forgiveness and take action to better fulfill this responsibility.

Reflect on the **Word**

- As we have seen, in 1 Chronicles, the line of David is highlighted because from it will come the Messiah.

- Today, we read a list of names from the tribe of Levi. God has promised the people a kingdom that will last forever—and worship that will give him glory for all time.

- Though priests come only from the tribe of Levi, David is sometimes described as wearing an *ephod*—a priestly garment—when he goes to pray before the Lord. (As we have seen, David is from the tribe of Judah.)

- Jesus, a descendant of David in the tribe of Judah, is described as a priest in the order of Melchizedek—which is different from the Levitical priesthood. Here, David foreshadows Jesus both as King and priest.

- In 2 Samuel 19, we see that David mourns the death of Absalom. This is understandable for him as a father, but it brings shame upon the people because of the twenty thousand who died to preserve David's kingdom. Seeing David's grief, the people believe he would rather they had died than Absalom.

- Sometimes, sorrow and personal loss can get in the way of the love we need to show to those in our lives. While we can grieve, we still need to love.

- Later, the people of Judah reestablish David as the king of Israel, but there is dissension between them and the other tribes. Here, we can see the seeds of rebellion that will take place after the death of David's son Solomon.

- In 2 Samuel 19, it is clear that David does not want to assert himself as king; rather, he wants the tribes of Israel to receive him back wholeheartedly and affirm his kingship.

Take It to **Prayer**

Father in heaven, we give you praise today and every day. Your mercies are new every morning, and you speak to us with your fresh voice, your eternal voice, your voice that is the same yesterday, today, and forever—because your Word, Lord God, your Word, Jesus Christ, is the same yesterday, today, and forever. And so we thank you, and we give you praise today. Thank you for speaking to us words of knowledge, words of wisdom, words that even capture the penitence of our hearts, the sorrow of our hearts when we experience opposition, when we experience even internal failure. In Psalm 38 today, Lord God, you give us words of repentance, words that voice confidence in you when we need you the most and when we deserve you the least. And that's when you give us your love. That's when you give us your mercy—when we need it the most and deserve it the least. And so we give you praise and thank you in Jesus' name. Amen.

Dive **Deeper**

Illustration and caption from Ritmeyer Archaeological Design

KING'S SEAT

This photograph shows the king's seat in the gate of Dan, in the north of Israel. The round stones at the corners held wooden posts supporting a canopy. The king's seat in Mahanaim may have looked similar. (See 2 Samuel 19:8.)

Reflect on the **Word**

- 1 Chronicles 25 speaks of the Temple musicians: the sons of Asaph, Heman, and Jeduthun. Psalm 39 is a psalm associated with Jeduthun.

- In 2 Samuel 19, David is hailed as the king of Israel. All the tribes are competing to see who can honor him more as he crosses the Jordan—and they resent the men of Judah because they are accompanying David.

- In 2 Samuel 20, Sheba, son of Bichri, a member of the tribe of Benjamin (from which Saul came), claims that he is the new king. Some tribes choose to follow him rather than David. Here we see the fickleness of the human heart.

- Sheba is defeated. When Joab is about to destroy the city where he has retreated, a wise woman there says that they will hand Sheba over if Joab spares them.

- As we see in 2 Samuel 20:3, violence begets violence. David left ten of his concubines behind to care for the house, and Absalom raped them. Because of this, David treats them as widows. They are sequestered until their deaths. This seems unjust. They are "caught in the crossfire" between David and Absalom's evil choices.

- Here we see how others can suffer due to our sins. The consequences of our evil choices do not end with us.

- We need to reflect on how others have been affected by our sins. We can face this difficult truth with God's grace and with the support of one another.

Take It to **Prayer**

Father in heaven, we give you praise, and we thank you. We know that you love us, and we know that we can trust in your love for us even in the midst of darkness, even in the midst of failure, even in the midst of discipline. Lord God, as Psalm 39 says, even when your hand is heavy upon us, even when your hand is heavy upon us in discipline, in correction, we know that we can trust you. Help us to see your fatherhood in your discipline, to not give in to the temptation to see a tyrant when you are actually a good Father—to not see a dictator when you are actually a good dad. But help us to receive the discipline that you allow to come our way, to receive the discipline that you bring into your lives so that we can have a change of heart, so that we can have a change of direction, so that we can become more and more like you, our God, our Father, our dad. In Jesus' name we pray. Amen.

Dive **Deeper**

When we sin, the consequences of our bad choices are not usually limited to us. How often have others suffered because of our sins? Take this question to prayer and ask God for the grace to face the truth and seek his will.

Reflect on the **Word**

- In 1 Chronicles 26, we see the division of the gatekeepers for the Temple area. Psalm 84:10 says, "I would rather be a doorkeeper in the house of my God than dwell in the tents of wickedness." It is remarkable that God gives such honor to those who guard the doors of the Temple.

- Some holy monks and consecrated religious served as porters of their monasteries—they were tasked with remaining by the door and letting people in and out.

- Everything we do, when we do it for the Lord, is sanctifying.

- In 2 Samuel 21, we read that there is a three-year famine. God reveals that the famine is taking place because Saul had killed Gibeonites. About four centuries before David's reign, the Israelites had sworn never to harm the Gibeonites, and the Lord expects them to keep their promise.

- The Gibeonites request that David deliver seven members of Saul's family to be executed. This is yet another example of how others can suffer due to our sins. Here, others suffer because of the sin of Saul.

- The final section of 2 Samuel 21 describes wars with the Philistines.

- There is something powerful about how David, despite being old and weary, is still willing to go into battle. In 2 Samuel 11, we see that he avoided battle, but now he is willing to do his duty as king.

- David has to come face-to-face with the fact that he is no longer the man he once was. This is a lesson to all of us as we continue to grow and get older. There is something humbling about this truth.

Take It to **Prayer**

Father in heaven, we thank you, and we give you praise. And it is true that sacrifice and offering you do not desire. You have given an open ear and an open heart. What you desire is obedience. What you desire is for us to have a heart like yours. What you desire is mercy, not sacrifice; obedience, not sacrifice, in so many ways—that when we do offer you sacrifice, it is only out of obedience. It is always as simply a gift to you and done in response to your invitation. Lord God, we ask that you please always, always make us obedient to you. Help us to always say yes to you and to never, ever stop saying yes. And even in the moments of disaster, even moments where we have said no to you, even moments of great sin in our lives, help us in that moment to take the very next good step—that next good step being to simply say yes once again. Help us to say yes to you and to never stop saying yes. In Jesus' name we pray. Amen.

Dive **Deeper**

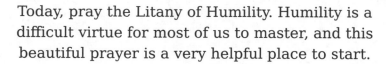

Today, pray the Litany of Humility. Humility is a difficult virtue for most of us to master, and this beautiful prayer is a very helpful place to start.

Reflect on the **Word**

- We will soon transition from the life of David to that of his son Solomon.

- 2 Samuel 22 is similar to Psalm 18. This is a psalm of David written early in his kingship, soon after he has been delivered from Saul and his enemies.

- David reflects on his life and proclaims that the Lord has saved him because he loves him. He can look back on his life and rejoice, despite all of his failures.

- At a certain point, we need to look back on our lives and see not only the victories but also the defeats—and be grateful to the Lord for redeeming us from our failures.

- David understands his brokenness. His sins have been on full display to the people of Israel. Yet he knows that God's strength has helped him and made him great.

- The challenge for us is to acknowledge the truth of our lives courageously, both the good and the bad, and recognize where God has helped us with his grace to overcome our weaknesses.

- We always need to choose praise and gratitude for God's loving mercy and forgiveness—and avoid choosing resentment and discouragement.

Take It to **Prayer**

Father in heaven, we do give you praise, and we do give you glory. We bless your name. We praise your name. Holiness and all glory is yours. All praise and thanksgiving belong to you for who you are and for what you have done in our lives. So, Lord, preserve us from resentment. Preserve us from corruption. And preserve us from despair and discouragement. Help us to be filled with your courage, to be filled with your grace, and therefore to be able to let our lives be signs of praise and signs of thanksgiving. In Jesus' name we pray. Amen.

Dive **Deeper**

***Who is the author** of the book of Psalms?*

Several individuals are traditionally considered the authors of the book of Psalms. These include David, Solomon, Moses, the sons of Korah, and Asaph. While we cannot know for certain that David wrote Psalm 23, for example, we have reasons to believe that what tradition holds concerning the authorship of the Psalms is correct.

In *A Catholic Introduction to the Bible: The Old Testament*, biblical scholars John Bergsma and Brant Pitre state that both the Septuagint (the Greek translation of the Hebrew Scriptures, from the third century BC) and the Dead Sea Scrolls attribute the Psalms to David and these other authors. They also point out that Jesus, in Matthew 22:41–46, quotes Psalm 110 and attributes it to David.

Scripture is truly the Word of God, with the Holy Spirit inspiring its human authors to write only what God intended to reveal (see CCC 105–106). While we cannot know for certain that particular psalms were actually written by David and others, or merely credited to them, we know that they are divinely inspired because they are part of the canon determined by the Church.

–Kara Logan

Reflect on the **Word**

- In 1 Chronicles 28, we read that David hands the reins over to Solomon.

- Though Solomon starts out strong, he will not end strong. Solomon starts out with great wisdom, but he will eventually waste that wisdom and turn his back on the Lord.

- But the Lord does not turn his back on his people. The same is true for us: when we turn our backs on the Lord, he does not abandon us.

- In 2 Samuel 23, we hear the stories of David's three mighty men: Josheb-basshebeth, a Tah-chemonite; Eleazar, son of Dodo, son of Ahohi; and Shammah, son of Agee the Hararite.

- David recognizes that he needed those around him to accomplish what God had called him to do; he knows that he could not have done it on his own.

- Like David, we should give God praise in every circumstance—and also recognize those around us and praise them for what they have done.

- Today, let us ask God to help us give what we have to give.

Take It to **Prayer**

Father in heaven, we give you praise. We do give you praise in all things. And God, thank you so much for Psalm 42. We are reminded that we can ask the question, "God, where are you?" Actually, we are not only reminded that we have the question "Where are you?"—we get so often assaulted by that question: "Where is your God? If you believe in him and if he is there for you and if he loves you, then point him out to me. Where is he?" Lord God, in those moments, we might be our own accuser. The evil one might be the accuser, or those around us might be the accusers that ask that question. And yet, in this moment, Lord, we know where you are; you are with us. Who you are for; you are for us. And you are beside us at all times. Lord God, we give you praise, and we thank you, and we make that declaration of faith. That declaration of faith that is even when it is hard for us to know where you are, or hard for us to sense your presence, we have faith. We have faith that you are faithful to your promises and you have said that you will be with us forever. You are with us at all times. Without you, we can do nothing. And so with you, we can do all things. Father, keep us close to you and never let us be parted from you. In Jesus' name we pray. Amen.

Dive **Deeper**

Like David, we should recognize and praise those around us. We should also help them however we can. Today, ask God to help you give what you have to give.

Reflect on the **Word**

- In the book of Numbers, we see how the Lord orders a census to help save his people, but David conducts a census to assert ownership over God's people.

- When he recognizes his sin, David is humbled, which shows that his heart is open to being converted. In repentance, he offers sacrifice to the Lord on behalf of the people.

- It is important for us to recognize that the Lord does not cause or tempt us to sin.

- 1 Chronicles 29 says that David gives freely and wholeheartedly of his wealth—all the things he has won in battle. Because of this, the people of Israel also give freely and wholeheartedly to the Lord.

- This brings joy to David because it brings joy to the Lord.

- We bring joy to the Lord when we give joyfully and without resentment.

- We need to ask ourselves: How can we love the Lord with whole hearts? How can we give joyfully to the Lord, not just out of our excess, but out of our need?

Take It to **Prayer**

Father in heaven, we do give you thanks, and we give you praise. It is true that weeping may last for the entire night. Weeping may last for an entire season. Weeping may last for so long. But joy truly does come with the morning. Joy truly does come with the rising of the sun. And joy comes even in the midst of grief, with the rising of your Son, Jesus Christ. Lord God, we know that we are faithful to you when it suits us. Help us to be faithful to you at all times. We are faithful to you in good seasons, and we ask you to please help us to be faithful to you in all seasons. We make this prayer in the name of Jesus Christ, our Lord. Amen.

Dive **Deeper**

Today, identify one way that you can give freely
and joyfully to the Lord—and do it!

Reflect on the **Word**

- Today's reading from 1 Kings indicates a transition. We are getting to the end of David's life.

- Through the rest of the books of Kings, we will hear about numerous kings, many of whom do not follow the Lord.

- Adonijah, one of David's sons, wins many people over and declares himself king, so Bathsheba, Solomon's mother, goes to David and tells him this has happened.

- As we have seen, David is a success in every area of his life except with his own family. If he had been paying attention, he would have seen this betrayal coming.

- In 2 Chronicles 1, we read that Solomon asks the Lord for wisdom.

- We might ask how Solomon starts out wise and later falls away from God. The problem begins when he starts amassing treasures. In direct disobedience to Deuteronomy, he collects horses from Egypt.

- While wisdom is a great virtue to have, obedience is more powerful. Disobedience to the Lord will be Solomon's downfall.

- All of us have been given gifts from God—but they mean nothing unless we use them to accomplish his will.

Take It to **Prayer**

Father in heaven, we give you praise. We give you glory and honor. There is no reason when you are with us, when you are near us, for our souls to be cast down. Yes, Lord God, we experience grief. We experience suffering. We experience loss in this life and in this world. And so our hearts can be broken. But, in all things we can still have joy. We can still have this abiding and pervasive sense of well-being because we know who you are. We know your character. We know your heart. We know your steadfast love for us. Because of that, Lord God, we can have that abiding and that pervasive sense of well-being. We can have joy in all circumstances. That even when our hearts are broken, even when our souls are tormented, even when our bodies are wracked with pain and grief, that we do not have to be cast down, because you are with us. And you are for us. And if you are for us, who can be against us? We give you praise, Lord God. So thank you. Thank you. Help us, bolster us up, and strengthen us, Lord God. Especially when the grief gets too big, when the suffering gets to be too much, when this day is overwhelming, strengthen us. Help us take one step forward. Help us take the next good step. In Jesus' name we pray. Amen.

Dive **Deeper**

Why was Solomon selected from among all of David's sons to be his successor? Did Bathsheba have something to do with this?

When King David's son Adonijah makes himself king, the prophet Nathan asks Bathsheba to remind David of his promise that her son, Solomon, would be king. When Bathsheba does so, David orders Zadok the priest and Nathan to anoint Solomon ruler over Israel and Judah.

Here we see Bathsheba's power of intercession. Since she is the mother of the king (the *gebirah*, in Hebrew), Bathsheba becomes queen. A little later, in 1 Kings 2, we will see that she, as queen mother, intercedes during her son's reign as well. In this way, she is a type of Mary, Queen of Heaven and Earth, who intercedes for us with her Son, Jesus, the King.

–Kara Logan

Reflect on the **Word**

- Today, we hear David's final words to Solomon. He imparts his hard-earned wisdom to his son.

- David tells Solomon that there will be people who will seek to get close to him to take advantage of him—and that he will need to deal with them in a just way. In the rest of 1 Kings 2, we read how Solomon attempts to mete out this justice.

- We often hear that children pay more attention to the example we set than the advice we offer. David advises Solomon to stay close to the Lord and heed his commands, but his example to his son was that of a divided heart and a distant father.

- We will soon see that Solomon follows his father's example rather than his advice.

- Adonijah asks Bathsheba to have Solomon give Abishag the Shunammite to him as his wife. Since Abishag is one of David's concubines, this is a power play by Adonijah, a last-ditch effort to usurp the throne.

- In the previous chapter, we saw Bathsheba bow in the presence of David. Here, though, King Solomon rises to meet Bathsheba and bows to her. We read that there is a throne for her to the right of his. Since the king has many wives, his mother is the queen of the kingdom.

- The Church on earth and in heaven is the fulfillment of the kingdom of Israel. In this new kingdom, Jesus is the king and Mary is the queen.

- We give Mary honor—not worship—because Jesus himself gives her honor.

Take It to **Prayer**

Father in heaven, we give you praise, and we do thank you. Yes, to you, Lord God, belongs steadfast love. To you belongs power. You love us with a love that doesn't change. You love us with a love that is constantly dynamic and constantly activated. Lord God, you are not a God of potency, you are a God of actuality. You are not a God of dreams, you are a God of reality. And in all things we trust you. In all things we praise you. And this day, as you speak to us once again, we continue to trust in you. Please hear our prayer and please make yourself known by every one of us. In Jesus' name we pray. Amen.

Dive **Deeper**

Today, honor Mary according to Jesus' own example. Pray the Rosary, asking for her intercession in your life, or praise God with her by praying the words of the Magnificat in Luke 1:46-55.

Reflect on the **Word**

- In today's reading from 2 Chronicles, we see the greatest work of Solomon's life—the building of the holy Temple of the Lord.

- We read how the Levites carry the Ark of the Covenant into the sanctuary of the Temple. This solemn act is honored by the Lord, and the glory cloud fills the space.

- Solomon prays for wisdom at Gibeon, the former place of worship before the Temple was built. His sacrifice is a sign that he is giving his heart to the Lord.

- At the beginning of 1 Kings 3, we see that Solomon marries a daughter of Pharaoh. This shows how Solomon will increase his own family and enter into alliances with the surrounding nations.

- For the first time, we begin to sense that Solomon, for all his wisdom, is going to do something unwise.

- The Lord has given Solomon the wisdom to *know* the difference between right and wrong, but he does not necessarily *choose* what is right over what is wrong.

- Like Solomon, we might know the right thing to do, but this does not mean that we will always do the right thing.

- We need God's grace both to *know* the truth and *choose* to live it.

Take It to **Prayer**

Father in heaven, we thank you for your Word. We thank you for revealing your heart to us. We thank you for continually turning our hearts to you because our hearts can be so easily turned away from you. And so, Lord, in this moment right now, God, I just want to speak to you about this psalm that we just prayed and how clearly the righteous find a place in your temple, how the righteous find a place in your heart, how the righteous find a place in you. And Lord, so often we are not righteous. So often we are the opposite of that. We are unrighteous. We are false. We are fickle. We are sinners. And yet, you still take us back even then. Even when we are not righteous. Even when we are disasters. You still love us. And you never give up on us. Help us to never give up on you. In Jesus' name we pray. Amen.

Dive **Deeper**

Knowing the right thing is one thing; choosing to do it is another. Pray for the grace to know *and* choose the truth in all areas of your life today.

Reflect on the **Word**

- Solomon delegates his authority by selecting twelve men to serve as leaders in Israel.

- As Catholics, we can see ourselves as members of the universal Church; other times, though, we might think in more territorial or "parochial" ways—"I go to St. Martin's. I would never go to St. Luke's."

- While we belong to our parishes, we always need to remember that we belong to a universal Church.

- In 2 Chronicles 6, we see a big shift in the way worship takes place. Solomon establishes the Temple in Jerusalem as the sole place of sacrifice.

- We will soon see how the kingdom of Israel becomes divided.

- Despite political division, worship in the Temple is what unites all of God's Chosen People and gives them their identity.

Take It to **Prayer**

Father in heaven, yes, all creation, all of creation praises your name. All of creation gives you glory. Father, the fact that we can look around this world that you have made with all of its danger, with all of its distress, but with all of its power and beauty and even mere existence ... it all gives praise to you. It all gives you glory. It all points back to you, the Creator of this incredible creation. And so we give you thanks, just like David, who wrote Psalm 65. We give you thanks. Thanks for earth's bounty. Not only is this earth beautiful, this earth provides for us. And so, God, we give you thanks. And we actually also ask you to give us wisdom like you gave wisdom to Solomon to be able to know how to live in this world, how to live in this earth—how to not only give thanks to you for creation, but also how to use this creation in a way that honors you, that honors the gift, and that helps our neighbor. Not just our neighbor that exists, but our neighbor in the future, Lord God. You have made all creation for us, for our ancestors, and also for our descendants. And so help us. Give us wisdom to be able to know how to live in this world so we can pass it on to the next generation. But we give you thanks. In all things, Lord God, we give you thanks. In Jesus' name we pray. Amen.

Dive **Deeper**

Today, pray for the Church, both for the members of your parish and for Catholics throughout the world.

Reflect on the **Word**

- In 2 Chronicles 7, we hear how God responds to Solomon's prayer of dedication of the Temple. God demonstrates the power of his presence by sending fire down from heaven.

- The Temple is essential because the presence of the Lord will abide there and it is where the people will offer worship.

- As we have seen, we must worship God in the manner he wants us to worship him.

- The Lord tells Solomon that he will be with him, as he was with David, his father—if he follows him. If he serves other gods, however, God will "pluck him from the land."

- Though the Lord has given Solomon a direct warning to remain close to him, we know that he does not.

- Solomon takes foreign women as his wives, but instead of bringing them into the covenant, he allows them to continue to worship their false gods. This opens Solomon up to idolatry.

- The worship God desires is obedience. While Solomon is the wisest man in Israel, he is unwilling to be obedient to the Lord.

- There is only one way to love God: to obey him and love our neighbor.

Take It to **Prayer**

Father in heaven, we give you praise. You do hear our prayers. God, every time we talk to you, Lord, you hear our voices. You know the longing of our hearts. You know the depth of our prayer. You also know our distraction. You know how easily we can be distracted from loving you with our whole heart, with our whole mind, with our whole strength. You know how easily it is that we are turned aside from you. And so we thank you for being able to hear through all the noise, cutting through all of the distraction, cutting through all of the turmoil that our hearts can experience—because you know our hearts. You not only know the peace in our hearts, you know the troubled hearts that live in our chests. And so we ask you, please once again, let your ears be open, let your eyes be open to see who we are, to see us truly and to hear our voice and to hear our prayers this day and every day. We make this prayer in Jesus' name. Amen.

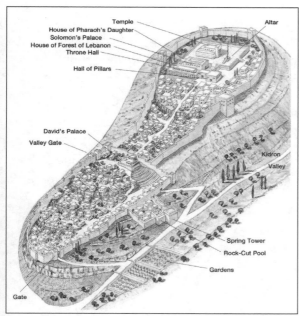

Illustration and caption from Ritmeyer Archaeological Design

Dive **Deeper**

JERUSALEM AT THE TIME OF SOLOMON

This reconstruction drawing shows Jerusalem at the time of Solomon. Solomon built the Temple to the north of the City of David, on top of Mount Moriah. (See 2 Chronicles 3:1.)

Reflect on the **Word**

- We read in 1 Kings 6:7 that as the Temple is being built, the stone is prepared at a quarry. This is done "so that neither hammer nor axe nor any tool of iron was heard" there to ensure that a sacred silence is observed in the house of the Lord.

- The stone in the Temple is overlaid with wood, which is then overlaid with gold.

- This is interesting to note because only the priests are allowed to go into the inner sanctuary of the Temple to worship; the people never see its gold-laden furnishings. The Temple's glory is simply to honor the Lord.

- In the New Covenant, we enter into the sanctuaries of our churches. We get to see and participate in the beauty, which is intended to aid in our worship of God.

- In 2 Chronicles 9, we learn about the end of Solomon's life. Solomon built the Temple for the glory of the Lord. Now, though, we read that he amasses wealth for himself and his own glory.

- Here, we can ask whether Solomon is becoming an image of strength rather than actually being strong.

- We need to ask ourselves whether we are seeking to project an image of wisdom, holiness, or strength—rather than being truly wise, holy, or strong.

Take It to **Prayer**

Father in heaven, we thank you, and we give you praise. We thank you so much for the gift of your Word. We thank you for the gift of peace and deliverance, Lord God, because you do deliver us from our enemies. Now, even when we are in distress, even when it seems like the world is crashing around us, even when it seems there are obstacles—and truly there are obstacles in our lives—you make us lie down and sleep. Lord God, when we can't sleep, when we cannot find rest, when our minds are so busy, are so scattered, and we feel so stretched, so thin, then we can realize that we need to rely upon your grace and your mercy. God, when we pray, "Deliver me from this thorn. Deliver me from this trial," you speak to us the words that you spoke to St. Paul: "My grace is sufficient for you. Power is made perfect in weakness." And so, we acknowledge our weakness so that we can accept your power. And we know it's true: your grace is sufficient for every one of our days, for every one of our moments. And so we give you praise. In Jesus' name we pray. Amen.

Dive **Deeper**

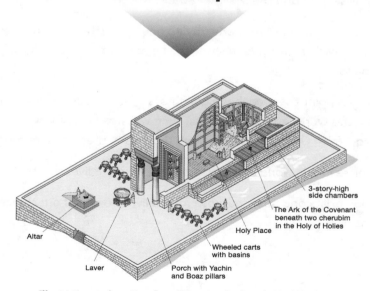

Illustration and caption from Ritmeyer Archaeological Design

SOLOMON'S TEMPLE

This reconstruction drawing of Solomon's Temple is based on archaeological evidence and the description in 1 Kings 6.

Reflect on the **Word**

- In our reading from Ecclesiastes, the "preacher" speaks of the vanity of created things. Here, the word translated *vanity* means something that is meaningless or like vapor or smoke.*

- We see that the wise one comes to understand that "there is nothing new under the sun" (Ecclesiastes 1:9).

- We might think that what we experience in our lives is new, but this is not the case. We are facing the same challenges people have always faced (though perhaps in different ways).

- In Ecclesiastes 2, the preacher decides to pursue self-indulgence and seek to maximize happiness. He soon discovers that this, too, is vanity because the human heart always wants more.

- He also pursues wisdom. However, he sees that while it is better to be wise, both the wise man and the fool meet the same end.

- We need to keep in mind that one day no one on earth will even know our names. If we are living for a legacy to be remembered, this is vanity, meaningless.

- The ultimate point the preacher highlights is this: If we are living in this world simply for this world, it is meaningless. Time will erase everything if we are living apart from God. But there is more than time; there is more than this life.

- If our choices in this world matter in eternity, then our lives matter.

- Only if God exists and has a purpose for our lives do any of our choices matter at all.

---

* Bible Hub, s.v. "1892. hebel," accessed September 10, 2021, biblehub.com.

Take It to **Prayer**

Father in heaven, we give you praise, and we thank you. And we do rise early, and we pray to you. And we listen to your Word, whether early or midday or whatever random time of the day, Lord God. We allow you to speak your Word to us. Your Word of the story of Solomon building his own home, and the Temple being constructed, and the Word of the Lord from Ecclesiastes coming face-to-face with the limits of human living—the limits of human life, the limits of human strength, power, wisdom, work, and memory. With you, Lord God, though, righteousness and goodness and justice endure forever. With you, Lord God, our works endure forever. Without you, we can do nothing. But with you, all things are possible. Help us to do all things with you and for you and for the glory of your name. In Jesus' name we pray. Amen.

Dive **Deeper**

Why is it so important *that the Temple be the only place where burnt offerings to the Lord are offered?*

It is important to emphasize that God must be worshipped in the way that he has commanded to be worshipped.

As we have seen in the periods of Patriarchs, Egypt and Exodus, and Desert Wanderings, burnt offerings were offered prior to the building of the Temple. However, God's presence dwelt in the Temple in a special way. The Temple contained the Ark of the Covenant, and the cloud of the presence of God filled it during its dedication (see 2 Chronicles 5:13–14).

The Temple was specially consecrated to God. After its completion, it was the only place where the Levitical priests could offer sacrifices to God. These offerings required special, consecrated vessels on altars dedicated for this task. If burnt offerings were offered outside of the Temple, this was considered idolatry. We will see this especially when the kingdom divides under Jeroboam, who establishes worship apart from the Temple. He makes two golden calves, ordains his own priests, and sets up separate feasts.

–Kara Logan

Reflect on the **Word**

- Today, in 1 Kings 8, we again see the Ark of the Covenant brought into the Temple for the first time, carried by the priests.

- Originally, the Ark of the Covenant contained the stone tablets of the Ten Commandments, manna, and Aaron's staff. At this point, only the tablets remain.

- As the Ark of the Covenant is brought into the holy place, the presence of God fills the Temple in such a powerful way that the priests are momentarily prevented from doing their tasks.

- In the book of Ecclesiastes, the "preacher" considers the passing nature of happiness on earth.

- The takeaway: we should have *plans* rather than *dreams*. In other words, we should set out to do what we say we will do.

- Ecclesiastes tells us that if we love money, we will never be satisfied with it. Many people make huge salaries but have no life outside of their work. They keep working harder, though, because they want to make even more money.

- We need to examine our own lives to see if we have a similar mentality regarding anything of this world. Where is something not enough, no matter how much of it we have?

Take It to **Prayer**

Father in heaven, we give you praise, and we thank you. We just ask that you please open your ears to our cry, open your eyes to our trouble, and, Lord God, open your hand in our need. You know what we need, and you hear our prayers always. You see us constantly, and yet you desire that we ask. You desire that we pray. You desire that we seek and knock and ask. And we ask that you please hear our prayer this day. See our need this day and open your hand to give us what we need. But also we ask you, Lord, to open our hands that we can receive from you. Open our eyes to be able to see you clearly and your will. And open our ears to hear your voice. We ask this in Jesus' name. Amen.

Dive **Deeper**

Consider the question "Where in my life is something not enough, no matter how much of it I have?" Bring this question to prayer and ask for the grace to know what truly matters.

Reflect on the **Word**

- Solomon, the wise one, comes to the end of his life in foolishness; the builder finishes his life in ruins. As we have seen, the Lord has told Solomon that he will establish his throne forever—if he does not turn away from him and serve other gods. Solomon does not take the Lord's words to heart, however.

- Ecclesiastes can be troubling and, at times, confusing, but it can also be inspiring if we receive it correctly.

- The author of Ecclesiastes says that the day of our death is more important than the day of our birth—meaning, all things will end. If we recognize this, then we can live with clarity and purpose.

- In Ecclesiastes 6, the author describes a man to whom God gives wealth and possessions but who does not have the ability to enjoy them. Many of us get trapped into worrying about so many things that we cannot find joy in the gifts we have been given.

- Ecclesiastes 7:10 advises us not to look back on the past and think that it was better than the present.

- Ecclesiastes 7:21 says not to heed everything people say about us, lest we hear something negative. In our hearts, we are aware we have spoken negatively about others. Wisdom comes in understanding this: since we do not necessarily mean much by our comments about others, we should not take others' comments about us to heart.

Take It to **Prayer**

Father in heaven, thank you so much. God, thank you so much. Thank you for your Word and thank you for your wisdom that you share with us. Thank you for allowing us to ask questions and to question reality. Thank you for letting us and inviting us to question goodness and question righteousness and question the mystery of evil and our own mystery of evil in our own hearts. Thank you for allowing us to come before you with all these questions and with all this brokenness that is not just around us but is also in us. Thank you for sharing your Word, the words of Qoheleth, the words of the "preacher," who gets to ask the big questions and invites us into asking those big questions. We give you praise, and we thank you in Jesus' name. Amen.

Dive **Deeper**

Why did Solomon *give Hiram twenty cities in Galilee?*

Solomon was known as the master builder of the Old Testament. He built not only the palace of the king but the Temple in Jerusalem as well. The Lord warned the Israelites that an earthly king would claim ownership of their land, levy taxes on them, and put their children to work. The massive construction efforts that were required in building the Temple and the palace fulfilled the Lord's words.

Hiram, the Phoenician king of Tyre, supplied Solomon with cedar and cypress for the Temple. In return, Solomon gave Hiram twenty cities in Galilee as a gift—one city for each year the Phoenician king had supplied the materials. But the cities did not please Hiram. An interesting point is that, as we know, Jesus was from Nazareth in Galilee. The Gospels show that the sentiments of people in Jesus' day toward the towns of Galilee were not favorable: "Can anything good come out of Nazareth?" (John 1:46). So Galilee never got any respect, it would seem.

–Jeff Cavins

Reflect on the **Word**

- In our reading from 1 Kings today, we have a review of Solomon's life.

- While Ecclesiastes seems to portray a negative view of life, it is actually an honest assessment.

- In Ecclesiastes, we learn that God's ways are inscrutable. A sinner gets ahead while a righteous man does not—and yet they face the same fate.

- A main takeaway from Ecclesiastes is this: if this life is all there is, then all is vanity, all is meaningless because nothing endures.

- Ecclesiastes 9 tells the story of a poor wise man who delivers a city, yet nobody knows his name.

- Being at peace with the recognition that we will eventually be forgotten is a gift. Our lives matter because this life is not all there is.

- Even if I am the smartest or strongest person in the room, this is only by chance. Eventually this moment will end—and someone smarter or stronger will come along.

- In such moments, we are invited to surrender to the Lord rather than to give in to our desire to be in control. While we should want to be as strong, smart, and good as we can, ultimately all of us are called to surrender to the Lord in trust.

Take It to **Prayer**

Father in heaven, you are great and glorious. How majestic is your name? You have revealed your name to us, which boggles the mind, Lord God, and fills our hearts today. Not only do you have the majestic name, not only do you have the glorified name, but you have revealed your name to us. And you have also revealed what the psalmist says, what David says, that you can look at the world around us and the universe, the billions upon billions of stars, the space that you've created and yet, what is man that you care for him? Who are we that you are mindful of us, that you are constantly attentive to us? And yet you are, God, because you have made us in your image and likeness. And in Christ you have made us your children. And so we just thank you. Thank you so much for being attentive to us. Thank you so much for creating us. Thank you so much for sustaining us and redeeming us. Please receive our thanks this day, Lord, in Jesus' name. Amen.

Dive **Deeper**

Today, strive to surrender to God as you go about your daily tasks, asking him for the grace to give him control instead of trying to be in control yourself.

Reflect on the **Word**

- Our decisions have consequences, both for ourselves and others. David was an absent father who did not pass his relationship with the Lord on to Solomon. Though Solomon has been blessed with wisdom, he fails to be faithful to God.

- Solomon experiences an unraveling of his faith because he gives his heart to something other than the Lord—to hundreds of wives and concubines, as well as false worship.

- Solomon builds a beautiful Temple for the Lord, but he also builds temples for the gods of his pagan wives.

- One of the false gods Solomon honors is Molech, to whom child sacrifices are offered. He participates in this great evil not because he believes it to be true, but because he has given his heart away to the wrong people.

- This is why it is important to choose relationships that support rather than weaken our relationship with God. It is especially important to choose a spouse who shares our faith.

- The words of Ecclesiastes, this great wisdom book, should not make us lose hope but make us humble. As Ecclesiastes 12 says, the whole duty of man is to fear God and keep his commandments.

- We read that God will bring every deed, every secret thing, into judgment, whether good or evil.

- While we might not know the meaning of every moment, every moment has meaning.

Take It to **Prayer**

Father in heaven, yes, give us wisdom. Give us wisdom to number our days correctly. Give us wisdom to know who we are. Yesterday we prayed Psalm 8 of "Who are we that you care for us? Who are we that as human beings you even keep us in mind?" And now today, Lord God, we just are struck by our need to ask you please to be reminded of how we need you to care for us, how we need you to pay attention to us because of the fact that there are so many obstacles, there are so many battles, there are so many things that are facing us this day—that we just ask you for your grace and for your strength. We ask for your attentiveness and your love to be present in our lives, especially in the midst of battle, in the midst of struggle, in the midst of this life. We trust in you. We praise you. And we love you. Please receive this in Jesus' name. Amen.

Dive **Deeper**

Have you given your heart to someone or something other than the Lord? Reflect on this question today. If you have turned away from him, ask the Lord to reclaim your heart for himself alone.

Royal Kingdom **Recap**

The Royal Kingdom is a wondrous time in Israel's history. The twelve tribes are united as a nation and a permanent Temple is built in Jerusalem for them to worship the Lord. Although their lack of trust in God leads them to ask for a king like other nations, God grants their request. God makes a covenant with David, which will ultimately be fulfilled in Jesus.

Royal Kingdom **Review Questions**

Use these questions to test your knowledge of the time period you just finished. Answers are below. No matter how many you can answer, celebrate the accomplishment of finishing another period!

1. At the end of the Conquest and Judges time period, Israel asked for a king. Which prophet did God task with this request?

2. The first king of Israel was Saul. What tribe was he from?

3. How did the young David comfort King Saul when he was depressed?

4. How many stones did David have with him when he defeated Goliath?

5. What piece of his clothing did David cut off of Saul to show that he could have killed him had he wanted?

6. Who was the prophet who convicted King David about his adultery with Bathsheba?

7. The kings of Israel were warned that a king should not have many wives. How many wives did Solomon have?

7. seven hundred
6. Nathan
5. the corner of his garment
4. five
3. He played the harp (or, the lyre).
2. Benjamin
1. Samuel

Gold is the color of the **MESSIANIC FULFILLMENT** time period because it represents the gifts of the Magi.

Key **Events & Figures**

Mark is the shortest of the Gospels, and some scholars believe it was the first to be written. Mark's explanation of Jewish customs suggests that his Gospel was intended for Gentile Christians. Matthew, Mark, and Luke are called the "synoptic Gospels," as all three share similar content.

The first half of Mark's Gospel reveals the identity of Jesus as the long-awaited Messiah and Son of God (Mark 1:1–8:30). The second half focuses on the mission of Jesus (Mark 8:31–16:8). Mark teaches his audience that Jesus is the Son of Man and must suffer many things; be rejected by the elders, chief priests, and scribes; and be killed, after three days rising from the dead.

What **Changes?**

Israel had a long history of messianic figures, such as David and Judas Maccabeus, who resisted their political enemies. In the Gospel, Jesus changes this stereotypical mode of action by becoming a Suffering Servant, one who will be victorious by offering himself as the atoning sacrifice for the salvation of the world. Through his passion, death, and resurrection, Jesus overcomes the true enemy of humanity—sin.

Jesus' faithfulness to the will of the Father will become the model for his disciples. In contrast to picking up arms and fighting the political system of the day, Jesus calls all who follow him to deny themselves, pick up their cross, and come after him. What Mark proclaims is foolishness to some but life for those who both believe and walk in the truth.

Reflect on the **Word**

- Most scholars believe the Gospel of Mark is an account of the apostle Peter's experiences. It is thought that Mark was a companion of Peter.

- Written during the persecution of the emperor Nero, the Gospel of Mark shows what it means to be a disciple of Jesus. We are called to pick up our crosses and follow him daily—and, in times of suffering and oppression, we are called to have hope and trust in him.

- Why does Jesus ask John to baptize him? John's baptism is one of repentance, and Jesus is sinless. The water of baptism does not make Jesus holy; on the contrary, it is Jesus who makes the water holy.

- The voice of the Father is heard from heaven: "You are my beloved Son; with you I am well pleased" (Mark 1:11). When we are baptized, God says the same thing to us, as we become his adopted children.

- After Jesus' baptism, the Spirit immediately drives him into the wilderness for forty days to be tempted by Satan. He goes to battle against the Devil for us.

- Scripture tells us that, due to sin, the world is in slavery to the Devil. So Jesus comes not only to teach and heal us but to save us. We can either choose to belong to the kingdom of darkness by remaining in bondage to sin or we can be transferred by the grace of Christ into the kingdom of light.

- When Jesus tells the paralytic that his sins are forgiven, the scribes present claim that this is blasphemy because only God can forgive sins. Here we see in the Gospels that Jesus claims to be God.

Take It to **Prayer**

Father in heaven, we give you praise and glory. Thank you so much. Lord, thank you so much for revealing your Son to us. Thank you for giving your Son to us. You so loved the world that you gave your only Son, that all who believe in him might not perish but might have eternal life. And so we thank you, and we give you praise. Thank you for these next seven days. Thank you for this day where we just get to hear the words of the Gospel writer Mark. Thank you so much for giving to us the Good News, the opportunity to hear this Good News. So please receive our praise. Help us to be converted. Call us to be your disciples, to follow after you with all of our heart, mind, soul, and strength, and to love you with everything we are and everything we have. In Jesus' name we pray. Amen.

Dive **Deeper**

By your Baptism, you are an adopted son or daughter of God. In your time of prayer today, dwell on what this means and ask God for the grace to live in the kingdom of light.

Reflect on the **Word**

- Jesus, knowing that the synagogue elders are watching to see if he will heal on the Sabbath, asks them whether it is lawful to do good on the Sabbath. They remain silent, and Jesus looks on them with anger. They know the truth, but they are unwilling to acknowledge it in their pride.

- We always need to be ready and willing to speak the truth.

- Jesus shows that he is Lord over the Sabbath by fulfilling its intended purpose—bringing God's people into communion with him.

- Jesus speaks of the unforgivable sin—blasphemy against the Holy Spirit. Ultimately, this means being willfully unrepentant and refusing to accept God's mercy and forgiveness.

- We need to bring everything to the foot of the Cross and allow God to forgive us.

- When the Bible speaks of the "brothers" of Jesus, the term used refers to a male relative, not necessarily a blood brother.

- From the Cross, Jesus hands the care of his mother Mary to the apostle John. This would have been unthinkable if Mary had other sons.

- The whole point of the Gospels is to establish the identity of Jesus. After Jesus calms the storm, the apostles ask who he can possibly be. Jesus shows them that he is the Lord, the eternal Son of the Father.

Take It to **Prayer**

Father in heaven, we give you praise and thanks, and we just honor you and love you for the gift of your Son, Jesus, and for the gift of knowing here is his teaching, here is his heart, here is your heart, because he is the Word, the Word of the Father. And when we see him, we see you, Father in heaven. And so we thank you. We thank you for every one of these moments that we get. We thank you for every one of these clips, these images we have of Jesus here in Mark's Gospel. Thank you for Mark. Thank you for Peter, who taught Mark this. And thank you for you, Lord God, because you are deserving of all things and all praise in everything. In Jesus' name we pray. Amen.

Dive **Deeper**

***What is the unforgivable** sin of blasphemy against the Holy Spirit?*

In the Gospel, those whom Jesus is speaking of regarding this sin are so blind that they think the works of God are actually the works of the evil one. They do not see that they need repentance and forgiveness. They are not open to the Spirit working within their hearts. Why does Jesus say this sin is unforgivable when there is no sin that God will not forgive? Because this particular sin, in effect, prevents the Holy Spirit from working in one's life.

Regarding this passage, the *Catechism of the Catholic Church* states, "There are no limits to the mercy of God, but anyone who deliberately refuses to accept his mercy by repenting, rejects the forgiveness of his sins and the salvation offered by the Holy Spirit. Such hardness of heart can lead to final impenitence and eternal loss" (CCC 1864).

The unforgivable sin against the Holy Spirit, then, is being closed to the promptings of God, who urges us to repent and seek his forgiveness and mercy. In the end, it prevents one's true repentance due to pride.

–Kara Logan

Reflect on the **Word**

- In the exorcism of the Gerasene demoniac, Jesus sends the demons into a herd of two thousand pigs. For Jesus, one person is worth infinitely more than even two thousand pigs, though the pigs are valuable. This shows us how much the Lord cares for each of us.

- Since the Fall, we see brokenness upon brokenness because this world is now under the dominion of sin—of Satan. God shines a beam of light onto this brokenness.

- With every exorcism, Jesus takes back his Father's kingdom from the Evil One.

- Wherever the Gospel is proclaimed, it is always accompanied by exorcisms.

- During the Middle Ages, there were few exorcisms because so many infants were baptized early. We see a rise in exorcisms today because fewer people are being baptized—and even some baptized Christians have been denying the Faith.

- When Jesus tells the apostles to feed the hungry crowd that has accompanied them, they are confused. Clearly, they do not have enough food for several thousand people. But what little food they do have they bring to Jesus, who blesses it and tells them to distribute it to the people.

- This is what Jesus does for us, as well. We give Jesus what we have, he blesses it, and he gives it back to us so that we can offer it to others.

- When we find ourselves lacking in anything, Jesus tells not to be afraid to give him what we have.

Take It to **Prayer**

Father in heaven, we give you praise, and we exalt your name. We do sing and praise your power. And be exalted, Lord, in your strength, in your goodness, in your holiness—because you have revealed your deepest character. Your character is that you love us. Your character is that you are love. You don't just love us, God, you are love. And Father, Son, and Holy Spirit, you are an eternal exchange of love. Father, you so loved the world, once again we are reminded, you so loved the world that you gave your only begotten son so that all who believed in him might not perish but might have eternal life. You set us free. You set us free from slavery to sin and slavery to Satan, the Evil One. Help us to live in that freedom. Help us to live in your love. And help us to receive the grace of your redemption that you offer to us. In Jesus' name we pray. Amen.

Dive **Deeper**

When we give Jesus what we have, he blesses it and gives it back to us so that we can offer it to others. Nothing is too small or insignificant to give him. Today, give Jesus all that you have and ask how he wants you to offer it to others.

Reflect on the **Word**

- Jesus rebukes the Pharisees for rejecting the commandments of God in favor of their human traditions. For example, God commands them to honor their father and mother by taking care of their parents in their old age. Instead, some Pharisees make a donation to the Temple in their parents' name—exempting themselves from actually serving their parents.

- We are good at creating our own versions of what God is asking of us rather than doing what we *know* he wants.

- Mark 7 tells the story of the Syrophoenician woman who comes to Jesus, asking him to heal her daughter who is possessed by a demon. Jesus makes clear that he has come to save the Jews first. But he then shows that salvation comes through the Jews to the entire world.

- The woman persists in her request. She knows Jesus comes from God and that God loves all who belong to him. Like this woman, we do not approach God with a sense of entitlement. We do not deserve his grace; we know that it is a gift, freely given.

- When Jesus cures the deaf and the blind, he shows the power of the sacraments—sacred signs that convey God's grace to us through the material world. God becomes one of us, incarnate in human flesh, to save us. We receive salvation through our bodies, through the sacraments.

- Jesus brings the disciples to Caesarea Philippi and asks them, "Who do people say that I am?" Peter says that Jesus is the Christ.

- Peter then objects to Jesus' statement that he will suffer and be killed, but the Lord replies, "Get behind me, Satan!" (Mark 8:33). Peter is thinking in human terms and has become, at that moment, an obstacle to Jesus' fulfillment of God's plan.

- As disciples of Jesus, we are going to suffer for his sake. We are not going to fit in with the rest of the world. People will think we are backward or old-fashioned. But we cannot belong to Jesus without taking up our crosses and following him every day.

Take It to **Prayer**

Father in heaven, we give you praise, and we thank you. We thank you so much for being our divine shepherd, our Good Shepherd. Thank you so much for being the one who guides us, especially as we walk through the valley of the shadow of death. Lord God, that is what this world is. That is what life is. It is known as the "vale of tears." It is known as the valley of the shadow of death. And yet we can say, like David, "I fear no evil." Why? Because you are with me. Because you are with us. Your rod and your staff comfort us. Lord God, you can only be our Good Shepherd, really, if we are your sheep, if we allow you to direct us, if we allow you to guide us, if we allow you to protect us. But when we go wandering away from you, then not only are we left alone, not only are we vulnerable, not only are we in the valley of the shadow of death with no protection, we know that even then you come in search of us. David didn't know this. The ancient patriarchs, the prophets, didn't know this as clearly as we know this because, Lord God, through your Son, Jesus Christ, you have revealed that you are the One who seeks out the lost sheep. You are the One who, when we do wander, goes in pursuit of us, desperately seeking us. Because you have declared that for whatever reason you love us. And you pursue us even when we wander far from you. So, Lord God, pursue us. Now if we have wandered, pursue us, like the Good Shepherd that you are. And lead us back so that we may dwell in the house of the Lord forever all the days of our lives. In Jesus' name we pray. Amen.

Dive **Deeper**

Sometimes we are good at creating our own versions of what God is asking of us, like some of the Pharisees did, rather than doing what we know God wants. Examine the circumstances of your own life in prayer today. If there is an area in which you are not living in the way you know God wants you to, ask for the grace to follow his will.

Reflect on the **Word**

- Today, in Mark 9, we read about the Transfiguration. Moses and Elijah represent the Old Covenant—Moses represents the Law, and Elijah represents the Prophets. Jesus shows that he is not just another leader or prophet like Moses and Elijah. All of humanity will be judged by him.

- The apostles argue about which of them is the greatest. Jesus then teaches them that anyone who wants to be first must be last and the servant of all.

- The Lord warns his disciples of the grave consequences of giving scandal. Those with authority within the Church have a great responsibility to be holy and teach the truth faithfully.

- To those who would deny the reality of hell, Jesus makes it clear that it is real—and that it is possible for us to choose hell by our actions.

- Jesus is not suggesting we actually maim or harm ourselves when he speaks these challenging words: "If your hand causes you to sin, cut it off. If your eye causes you to sin, gouge it out." Rather, he is using this strong metaphor to indicate we must do whatever we can to get rid of whatever causes us to sin.

- In Mark 10, the Pharisees ask Jesus if it is lawful for a man to divorce his wife, saying that Moses permitted divorce in the Law. Jesus responds, "For your hardness of heart he wrote you this commandment. But from the beginning of creation, 'God made them male and female'" (Mark 10:5-6). Jesus makes it clear that divorce and remarriage are not part of God's plan.

- When a rich young man asks Jesus what he must do to inherit eternal life, Jesus responds, "Why do you call me good? No one is good but God alone" (Mark 10:18). He is inviting the man to reflect more deeply on what he is about to say: that he must sell all that he has, give to the poor, and follow him.

- Jesus has many teachings that seem difficult. They can be challenging and seem overwhelming. But he does not call us to do anything that he does not give us the grace and strength to do.

Take It to **Prayer**

Father in heaven, we give you praise. And we bless you, and you bless us, and you keep giving to us, and so we give you praise. And we know that you are the one who is blessed. Lord God, in the Gospel, you often ask, "What is it that you wish for? What is it that you want?" And if I don't know what it is that I want, if I don't know what it is that I wish for, if I don't know what is the deep desire of my heart, then I don't know how to answer this question. And so, Lord God, before I can even ask what I wish for, I ask that you please give us all a spirit of clarity, a spirit of actually knowing what it is that our heart longs for, knowing what it is that we really, truly desire. Because our hearts are clouded by misjudgment; our hearts are clouded by a number of contradictory desires. And so, Lord God, I don't even know what my heart wants half the time. And so I ask that you please ... before I can give you any answer of what it is that you want me to do for you, I need to know what it is. I need to receive a pure heart from you, a pure heart that can see not just other people well but also see what it is that is in the depth of my heart. God, I want to approach you always with clarity. I want to approach you always with confidence and with courage, and so I ask that you please send into my heart, and into the hearts of all those who are praying with me now, that spirit of clarity, of confidence, and of courage. In Jesus' name we pray. Amen.

Dive **Deeper**

Dwell on the teachings of Jesus in prayer today. Which teachings challenge you or seem overwhelming? Ask God for the grace to be faithful to these teachings.

Reflect on the **Word**

- In Mark 11 and 12, we read about the days leading up to Jesus' betrayal. Jesus has arrived in Jerusalem, where he faces his passion, death, and resurrection. The stakes are getting higher, and Jesus' teachings are becoming more pointed.

- When Jesus curses the fig tree, he is letting the people of Israel know that they must live like they are God's people. It is through them that he will bless the world. The Israelites are like the fig tree; they need to produce the fruit of belonging to the Lord.

- In Mark 12, we see the parable of the wicked tenants—who, again, represent the people of Israel.

- The key takeaway here is that a disciple of Jesus must bear fruit. If one does not bear fruit, then the question is whether he or she is a true disciple of the Lord. If we belong to Jesus, our lives should witness the fruits of the Spirit.

- When Jesus cleanses the Temple, he does so because his Father's house is intended to be a house of prayer. This is a metaphor for Baptism, when our souls become living temples of the Holy Spirit.

- We must allow ourselves to be cleansed by Jesus so we can glorify him in our bodies.

- The final part of Mark 12 presents us with the offering of the poor widow. The tithe is intended to be the first ten percent of one's income, whereas the widow gives everything.

- Both our firstfruits and our "final fruits" belong to God—everything from first to last. We have to ask ourselves how we can love God with our entire lives today.

Take It to **Prayer**

Father in heaven, you have blessed us. Lord, every single day you give us the blessing of a new day. Every single day you give us the blessing of your mercy. Your mercies are new every single morning, Lord God. And you give us a new day every single morning. A new day to honor you, a new day to know you better, a new day to let you love us. And that is, Lord God, it all comes down to this—it all comes down to: Will we let you love us? Will we let you be the Lord of our lives? Will we allow ourselves to reveal your image? And will we receive your inscription upon our hearts, that we love you with everything we have and everything we are and love our neighbors as ourselves? Lord God, help us first to be loved as fully as we possibly can by you. Help us to give you permission, once again, to love us this morning, to forgive us this morning, and to give us your grace. Help us to give you the permission to claim us as yours. In Jesus' name we pray. Amen.

Dive **Deeper**

We need to give God our firstfruits, our final fruits, and everything in between. Today, consider what giving back to God looks like in your life. Does it mean giving a higher percentage of your income to the Church? Does it mean giving generously of your time to a ministry at your parish? Does it mean serving others with a skill or talent you have? Make a realistic plan for how you can give to God.

Reflect on the **Word**

- In Mark 13, Jesus warns that the Temple will be destroyed. He also promises that those who follow him will be persecuted.

- This is true for the Church in every age. In some eras, many people are indifferent to Jesus and his Church, and in others, people and institutions are actively hostile toward the Church.

- Today, many families are divided over the teachings of Christ.

- Even in the midst of a culture that is hostile toward Christians, our call is to love the Lord as best we can and love those around us.

- We see that even in his last moments, Jesus is thinking of us and giving us the greatest gift he could give us on earth—the Eucharist.

- When Jesus prays to his Father in the garden of Gethsemane, he teaches us how we should pray—with honesty and trust.

Take It to **Prayer**

Father in heaven, yes, may you be blessed now and forever. Just like in Psalm 68, you led your people from Mount Sinai to Mount Zion. You led your people from Mount Sinai wrapped in cloud and wrapped in fire to Mount Zion, the Temple and your holy place where you dwell with your Holy Spirit—where you called your people to worship you. Lord God, you bring us today, even, into worship of you. You bring us today to the place where you dwell. You bring us today where your presence abides even as we hear today from Mark's Gospel. You are giving us the Last Supper; you are giving us Jesus' Body and Blood, Soul and Divinity in the Last Supper. Lord God, you have called us to worship you at the Mass, and we thank you for that gift. And we thank you for the gift of being willing to endure agony for us, endure humiliation for us, to enter into your passion for us. We don't deserve it. And yet, your love led you to the Cross. Your love for us and your love for the Father led you through Gethsemane. And we can only thank you with our prayers but also, Lord God, with our everything. With our everything may you be praised. In Jesus' name we pray. Amen.

Dive **Deeper**

Jesus shows us that prayer to the Father should be both honest and trusting. Take some time today to go to the Father in prayer honestly and with great trust in his love for you.

Reflect on the **Word**

- On the Cross, Jesus demonstrates that he intentionally experiences our pain out of love for us, taking upon himself our sins and the death those sins bring.

- The Cross reminds us of both the devastating effects of sin and the depth of God's love for us.

- To pay the cost for our sins, the Son of God gave his very life. It is not the nails that kept Jesus on the Cross but his love for us.

- On the Cross, Jesus says, "My God, my God, why have you forsaken me?" quoting the first line of Psalm 22. With these words, Jesus is not indicating that he has been abandoned by God; rather, he is pointing us to the entire psalm, which ends in a proclamation of deliverance.

- Jesus' crucifixion is not the end of the story. His glorious resurrection will soon follow.

- Psalm 22 praises the Lord and says that future generations will declare what God has done. As we read Mark 16, we get to declare what God has done.

- Jesus, the Son of God, has not only died for us; he is risen for us.

Take It to **Prayer**

Father in heaven, we give you praise. We thank you. Thank you so much. Thank you for giving us your Son. Thank you for giving us hope, because in the face of our own deaths, in the face of our own suffering and pain, in the face of our own sin, we have no hope if we are on our own. But Lord God, you have sent your Son to bear our sin. You have sent your Son to transform our suffering. And you have sent your Son to redeem the power of death, to conquer the power of death, and to transform it—to redeem death so that now death is no longer the enemy but death is our mother. And she gives birth to us in your presence. She brings us from this world into the next. She brings us from this life into eternal life with you. That's only possible because of your love, Father. Because of the love of your Son, Jesus Christ, and what he did for us—what he has done for us, and how he continues with you to send the Holy Spirit to be with us this day and every day. So Father, please, send your Holy Spirit upon us right now and transform in our hearts what needs to be transformed. Bring to life what is dead. Heal what is broken. And forgive, please, Lord God, forgive what is needing forgiveness. In Jesus' name we pray. Amen.

Dive **Deeper**

Pray the Stations of the Cross today and meditate on all that Jesus suffered for your salvation and the love he has for you.

Gospel of Mark **Recap**

In the Gospel of Mark, John the Baptist was the forerunner of Jesus. His proclamation of Jesus as the Lamb of God at the River Jordan inaugurated Jesus' public ministry. Jesus called twelve men to become his apostles and spend three years teaching and modeling the good news. As they followed Jesus, their hope of a new Israel faded as he was arrested, condemned, and crucified. Then, the Resurrection changed everything …

Gospel of Mark **Review Questions**

Use these questions to test your knowledge of the time period you just finished. Answers are below. No matter how many you can answer, celebrate the accomplishment of finishing this checkpoint!

1. Whom did Jesus heal in Peter's household?

2. What did Jesus do to the leper that astonished everyone?

3. Whom did the Pharisees accuse Jesus of eating with?

4. In Jesus' parable of the sower, what was the sower spreading?

5. Who did King Herod think that Jesus might be?

6. When Jesus triumphantly entered Jerusalem for the Passover, with what did the people greet him?

7. When the scribes asked Jesus what the greatest commandment was, how did he answer them?

7. Love the Lord your God with all your heart and love your neighbor as yourself.
6. with palm branches and garments spread before him
5. John the Baptist raised from the dead
4. the Word
3. sinners and tax collectors
2. Jesus touched the leper.
1. Peter's mother-in-law

Black is the color of the **DIVIDED KINGDOM** time period because it signifies Israel's darkest period.

Key **Events & Figures**

The period of the Divided Kingdom is the most complicated portion of the biblical narrative. The ten northern tribes are disgruntled by the way they are being treated by the king in the south. Jeroboam, the leader of the northern tribes, orchestrates a split away from the south resulting in two kingdoms, Israel and Judah.

In the Divided Kingdom, we need to pay close attention to the many kings of the north and the south. In addition, we need to be aware of the various prophets and to which kingdom they are prophesying.

This period shows that obedience to God and to the words of his prophets is critical for the people's survival. Faithfulness and holiness are center stage, but these become complicated by idolatry and power grabs. The message of the prophets who speak during this period is applicable to us today as well.

What **Changes?**

The Divided Kingdom, which has its roots in God's covenant with David, is relatively easy to understand. A king on the throne from the house of David is meant to be permanent. The monarchy, though, will be split between the northern kingdom (Israel) and southern kingdom (Judah) in 930 BC. The first king of the north is Jeroboam, while Rehoboam, the son of Solomon, rules in the south.

A critical issue for the northern kingdom is the people's lack of access to the Jerusalem Temple. They establish worship sites in Bethel and Dan centered around golden calves, along with their own feast days. This proves disastrous and ultimately ends in the Exile. During this period, the prophets warn both the north and south of their fate if they do not return to obedience to God and his word.

Reflect on the **Word**

- The people, including Jeroboam, come to Solomon's son Rehoboam, saying that Solomon made their lives difficult. Rehoboam seeks counsel from the old men, who tell him that the people will love him forever if he treats them well. The young men, though, say that he should treat them harshly.

- Where do we look for counsel? Do we look to those who agree with us or those who might have more wisdom or knowledge than we do?

- Rehoboam does not accept the counsel of the wise. Instead, he decides to follow the people who tell him what he wants to hear.

- Because of this, Jeroboam leads the ten northern tribes to secede and establish their own kingdom—Israel. The two southern tribes, Judah and Benjamin, become the kingdom of Judah.

- To keep the people from going to Jerusalem to worship in the Temple—which could turn them back to Rehoboam—Jeroboam establishes places of worship in Bethel and Dan in the Northern Kingdom. This is an act of idolatry. As a result, many Levitical priests move to Judah.

- The people of Israel are called to give God glory and to love him above anything else. God sends them prophets to call them back to fidelity to him, but they rarely listen to them.

- How often do we fail to listen to God's Word when he is clearly speaking to us?

- The Song of Solomon can be read as an allegory of the relationship between God and his people, as human love poetry, or as a foreshadowing of the union of Christ and his Church.

Take It to **Prayer**

Father in heaven, we give you praise and glory. We thank you for all these three books, for Kings, for Chronicles, and now for this first turn into the book of the Song of Solomon. We ask that you please open our hearts to be able to praise your name. Open our minds to be able to just grasp the reality of what happened with the divided kingdom of Israel and how that can happen in our own lives as well. Because without you, we are divided. Without you, we are always prone to fail. And so, be with us this moment and every moment. In Jesus' name we pray. Amen.

Dive **Deeper**

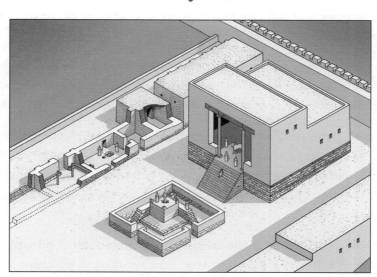

Illustration and caption from Ritmeyer Archaeological Design

JEROBOAM'S TEMPLE FOR IDOLATRY

After the kingdom of Solomon split, King Jeroboam placed golden calves in temples in Bethel and Dan to prevent the people from going to Jerusalem. (See 1 Kings 12:28-29.) This is a reconstruction drawing of the temple in Dan.

Reflect on the **Word**

- The Song of Solomon (or Song of Songs) is love poetry. In it, we see God pursuing us—Christ the Bridegroom is pursuing his Bride, the Church.

- As we see throughout the Song of Solomon, it is not that we have loved God but that he has loved us (see 1 John 4:10). We do not need to earn his love; he already loves us.

- 1 Kings and 2 Chronicles both tell the story of the division between the Northern Kingdom and the Southern Kingdom. A key theme here is faithfulness. When the people are faithful, they are blessed by the Lord; when they are unfaithful, bad things happen.

- Rehoboam has been unfaithful to the Lord. A prophet warns him when the Egyptian king seeks to attack Jerusalem, and Rehoboam repents. Jerusalem is not destroyed, but there are consequences to his infidelity. The enormous fortune amassed by his father Solomon and grandfather David has been lost in just a few years.

- After Rehoboam dies, his son Abijah is a good and faithful king. When he goes to battle with Jeroboam and the northern tribes, he does not rely on his own strength. He tells his opponents that they will never defeat the will of the Lord.

- In 1 Kings 13, a man of God warns Jeroboam against worshipping false gods. The man then refuses to share a meal, citing the Lord's instructions, but a prophet in Bethel invites him to dine, telling him falsely that an angel said it was OK. The man of God eats and drinks, and due to his disobedience to the Lord's command, the man is killed by a lion.

- A key theme in the period of the Divided Kingdom (and throughout the Old Testament) is this: When we know what God wants us to do, we need to do it—even when we are tempted to follow our own ideas. Faithfulness to the Lord is critical.

Take It to **Prayer**

Father in heaven, we give you praise, and we give you glory. We thank you so much for your Word and for continuing to speak to us and for continuing to pursue us. Lord, our hearts are broken, and yet you draw near to mend them. Our lives are full of darkness, and yet you bring your light into them. Heal what has been broken. Bring light to where there is darkness, and may everything that we do and everything we say and everything that we are give you praise and glory, now and forever. In Jesus' name we pray. Amen.

Dive **Deeper**

What is the Song of Solomon? Who wrote it?

Besides being a beautiful poem describing the love between man and woman and the goodness of romantic love, the Song of Solomon is a poetic allegory with three main interpretations.

1. The poem describes the love of God for his people, Israel. We see this imagery in the prophets, especially in Hosea, Isaiah, Jeremiah, and Ezekiel. When Israel is unfaithful, she is often described as a harlot, someone who is unfaithful to her one husband. On the other hand, God is the faithful husband who tries to woo back his unfaithful bride, Israel.

2. The Song of Solomon will also come to describe the relationship of Jesus Christ, the Bridegroom, for his Bride, the Church, in the New Covenant.

3. Saints have also taught that the Song of Solomon is an allegory of the love between God and every human soul. God is the ultimate Bridegroom of the soul.

Solomon is traditionally considered the author of this book, as well as several other books of the Bible's wisdom literature. There is evidence that some of these works could have been written later, but regardless of its authorship, the Song of Solomon is divinely inspired.

–Kara Logan

Reflect on the **Word**

- In the northern kingdom of Israel, the reign of Jeroboam is coming to an end. When his son Abijah becomes ill, Jeroboam sends his wife to Ahijah the prophet, who tells her that he will die.

- In desperate times, we need to turn to the Lord. Yet Jeroboam does not, so his kingdom comes to an end.

- As king of the Southern Kingdom, Judah, Rehoboam led the people into idolatry and other evils. Thankfully, his grandson Asa repents of many things his father and grandfather did. He destroys the idols and leads the people toward faithfulness to the Lord.

- Asa removes his mother, Maacah, as queen mother due to her infidelity to the Lord.

- This is an invitation for us to be faithful to the Lord in both our hearts and our actions.

- Do we have any idols that need to be removed from our lives? God wants our whole hearts; his love tolerates no rivals.

- God does not need sacrifices from us, but he does want us to be grateful for his gifts. We show our gratitude by giving him the "firstfruits" of our blessings.

- When we follow God's commandments, we are like the good king Asa, who follows the Lord faithfully in a world that is often opposed to him. This is possible only with the help of God's grace.

Take It to **Prayer**

Father in heaven, we praise you. Once again, we give you glory for the love you have for us and the desire that you have for our hearts. Lord God, on our own we offer so little to you. We offer nothing, almost nothing to you. And yet, even that little, even that nothing you receive with joy. You receive us in a way that we don't deserve. You pursue us and love us even to the point of giving up your own life so that we could have life, giving your Spirit into us so that we could be called truly your sons and daughters. And so, this day, help us to live in your love. Help us to receive that life. And help us to walk this day as your beloved sons and as your beloved daughters, because you are God, our Father. In Jesus' name we pray. Amen.

Dive **Deeper**

Today, bring the following questions to the Lord in prayer: *Do I have any idols that need to be removed from my life? Am I grateful for the blessings God has given me? Do I offer him my firstfruits?*

Reflect on the **Word**

- The Song of Solomon is a love song, using human love as an allegory for the covenant relationship between God and his people.

- The Song of Solomon says, "A garden locked is my sister, my bride" (Song of Solomon 4:12). A bride is first approached as a sister, as one who exists for her own sake, before a groom and bride give themselves to each other. This maintains the dignity of the person.

- As we will see in the books of Kings and Chronicles, the kings of Israel, the Northern Kingdom, are unfaithful to the Lord and lead the people into evil.

- The story of Asa, a good king, does not end well. Asa had been victorious against the Ethiopians—though his army was greatly outnumbered—because he relied on the Lord. But now he makes an agreement with the king of Syria, showing that he has placed his trust elsewhere instead of in the Lord.

- The seer Hanani tells Asa that, since he relied upon the king of Syria rather than the Lord, he will have to fight. Rather than accepting correction, Asa is angry and rebels against the Lord.

- While Asa has spent thirty-five years being faithful to the Lord, he abandons God in the final phase of his life.

- All of us have been called to be faithful to the Lord unto death—to finish well.

Take It to **Prayer**

Father, we give you praise, and we love you. Please receive our love. Please receive our praise. In Jesus' name we pray. Amen.

Dive **Deeper**

To learn more about St. John Paul II's Theology of the Body, watch Fr. Mike's Ascension Presents video called "Why God Gave Us Bodies."

Reflect on the **Word**

- In 1 Kings, we are introduced to Elijah and Ahab.

- Elijah hears the word of the Lord and obeys. Elijah's fidelity sets him apart—and offers an example for others to be faithful.

- He helps the widow of Zarephath, miraculously providing food for her and her son. He is inviting her to faithfulness.

- Elijah asks the people of Israel how long they will continue to waver between belonging to Baal and belonging to the Lord.

- Since they offer no response, he sets up a showdown between the prophets of Baal and the prophet of God, noting that the one who answers with fire is the true God.

- Unlike his uncommitted people, God is committed to his promises; he will answer. God is faithful, even when we are not. This sums up the entire story of the Bible. When God's people do evil, he is always ready to forgive them and restore them to a relationship with him.

- Jehoshaphat is a good king, but he makes a treaty with Ahab, the evil king of Israel.

- Jehu, son of the prophet Hanani, tells the king that this is wrong, as it helps those who hate the Lord. Jehoshaphat has set his heart on seeking God, though, as he shows when he destroys the Asherahs from the land.

Take It to **Prayer**

Father in heaven, we thank you. We thank you for your love for us. We thank you for the way in which you reveal to us how you work once again in history, how you work in our lives, how you work through ups and downs, and how you work through our faithfulness and even in the midst of our unfaithfulness. You don't abandon us. You don't give up. You continue to call us back to you. Help us to respond to that call with our whole heart, our whole strength, our whole might, our whole mind, and with everything we are. In Jesus' name. Amen.

Dive **Deeper**

The news that God is faithful—even when we are not—is life changing for us. Today, reflect on this truth in prayer, and ask for God's grace to be more faithful to him every day.

Reflect on the **Word**

- 1 Kings 19 tells the story of Elijah fleeing Jezebel. Even after the Lord's victory over the prophets of Baal on Mount Carmel, Elijah is discouraged and asks for death.

- We can be discouraged after victory because there are no more battles to fight. At this point, Elijah's ministry—his battle—is almost over, and discouragement sets in.

- But the Lord tells him, "Arise and eat" (1 Kings 19:5), giving him bread for the journey.

- In the sacramental rites of the Church, when a person close to death receives Holy Communion for the last time, it is called *Viaticum*—which means "bread for the journey."

- There will be a time in our lives when our best days on earth are behind us. But we still can look forward to eternity with God.

- Elijah goes to Horeb and meets the Lord—not in a storm, strong wind, earthquake, or fire, but in a still, small voice. God speaks to us in the quiet, but our lives are often so full of noise that we do not hear his voice.

- Elisha needs to leave his family and his former life behind to become a disciple of Elijah.

- We need to have a clear sense of God's promises—when we are faithful, the Lord fights for us.

Take It to **Prayer**

Father in heaven, we give you thanks, and we give you praise for this opportunity to just enter into the history of the kings, the history of the chronicles, the history of the family of Jesus, the history of the people you have chosen with their flaws and their faults, with their disasters and with their victories. Because we know that you are the God of our flaws and the God of our faults. You are the God of our disasters, and you are the God of our victories. And so we give our hearts to you this day and every day. Please receive them. Please receive our lives, our victories, and our defeats—our flaws and everything we are. In Jesus' name. Amen.

Dive **Deeper**

Eventually, all of us will face our final day on this earth. Today, pray for those who are close to death today. Ask that the Lord will grant them his strength, comfort, and salvation.

Reflect on the **Word**

- Remember God's threefold promise to Abraham: kingdom, worldwide blessing, and land. In the Old Testament, then, one cannot simply sell his land because it does not belong to him. The land has been divided up among the tribes. Naboth understands that he cannot sell his land. He is faithful.

- Ahab shows his heart, and Jezebel shows her heart. She sends letters in Ahab's name to incite the elders and nobles against Naboth, accusing him of wrongdoing. As a result, he is stoned to death.

- It has been said that evil only triumphs when good people do nothing. In the case of Naboth, the elders and nobles go along with the evil proposed by Jezebel.

- In the south, Jehoram, son of Jehoshaphat, kills all of his brothers. He sets up altars for false worship, placing his people in a position of vulnerability due to their infidelity to God, who had been protecting them when they were faithful. He follows the evil influence of his wife, the daughter of Ahab.

- After Jehoram dies, his son Ahaziah becomes king. He is wicked, following the example of his mother Athaliah.

- After the death of Ahaziah, Athaliah seizes the throne and destroys the entire royal family of Judah.

- God promised he would bless the world through the line of Abraham and that David's descendant would sit on the throne of Judah forever. Jeho-shabe-ath, daughter of Jehoram, hides Ahaziah's son Joash away for six years. We will discover what happens when his presence is revealed.

Take It to **Prayer**

Father in heaven, we are the object of your love, and you are eternal and mysterious, omniscient, omnipresent, and all-good, and yet you love us. You pursue us. You desire us. Even in our brokenness, even in our weakness, Lord, you still choose us. And so, we ask you as we always do—we ask you to help us to give you permission to be chosen by you. And help us to choose you back. Help us to receive your love. And help us to love you in return. In Jesus' name we pray. Amen.

Dive **Deeper**

What is the significance of sackcloth?

As we read in 1 Kings 21:27, when King Ahab hears the words of Elijah the prophet that God will punish him because of his evil ways, he "tore his clothes, and put sackcloth upon his flesh, and fasted and lay in sackcloth, and went about dejectedly." The Lord responds to the prophet Elijah regarding King Ahab's penance, "Have you seen how Ahab has humbled himself before me? Because he has humbled himself before me, I will not bring the evil in his days" (1 Kings 21:29).

Sackcloth is often mentioned in the Scriptures as a sign of repentance. When someone is mourning, fasting, offering sacrifice, or praying for a special intention, he often wears sackcloth. Since this cloth is rough against the skin, it is extremely uncomfortable to wear. In this way, the use of sackcloth shows that one is making reparation for sins committed. It is also a sign of humility, for it is the clothing of the poor.

Clothing should be a sign of our interior disposition and fit the occasion. While sackcloth is not typically used in the Church today to show repentance or mourning, we still perform exterior signs of repentance, including fasting, wearing ashes on our foreheads on Ash Wednesday, and wearing black (or a dark color) to a funeral.

–Kara Logan

Reflect on the **Word**

- 1 Kings 22 reiterates what we saw in 2 Chronicles.

- In 2 Chronicles 23, we read about Athaliah—daughter of Ahab, wife of Jehoram, and mother of Ahaziah—who makes herself queen and kills the royal family of Judah to eliminate any claim to the throne.

- For six years Athaliah reigns as queen, not knowing that Joash, one of Ahaziah's sons, has been hidden away.

- As the Lord promised David, it is from the line of Judah that the ultimate king will come. So the priests crown Joash king of Judah, and Athaliah is killed.

- The priest Jehoiada makes a covenant between himself, the people, and the king to be the Lord's people.

- Joash is only seven when he begins his reign, but he has good people influencing him. After the infidelity of Athaliah, the people return to a measure of faithfulness to the Lord under Joash.

- As we follow these events, we see again God's promise that he will remain faithful even when his people are not.

- This is true for each of us as well. We are not always faithful sons or daughters of our heavenly Father, but he is always a faithful Father.

Take It to **Prayer**

Father, we know that it is true. For stern as death is love. Love is as strong as death. Devotion is relentless as the netherworld. And so, we recognize that not only is love as strong as death, but love led you, God, to death for us, for our sake, in pursuit of us—so that you could draw us near to your heart, so that you could make us your children, so that you could love us in the way that you desire to love us. Love is as strong as death. And so we pray. Set me as a seal. Set me as a seal upon your heart. Set me as a seal upon your arm. Help us live every day as yours, as your beloved. In Jesus' name we pray. Amen.

Dive **Deeper**

Consistency is the foundation of faithfulness.
Watch Fr. Mike's Ascension Presents video called
"Consistency Will Make You Holy" for advice on
being consistent in your life.

Reflect on the **Word**

- In Psalm 69 we have a great prayer of deliverance from persecution, as well as a foreshadowing of Jesus on the Cross: "They gave me gall for food, and for my thirst they gave me vinegar to drink" (Psalm 69:21).

- How can we understand the psalmist when he says that he wants to see his enemies suffer in front of him? The key is to see this in spiritual terms: The enemies here are those of the soul, not other people but evil spirits. As St. Paul says, "For we are not contending against flesh and blood, but against the principalities, against the powers ... against the spiritual hosts of wickedness" (Ephesians 6:12). The enemies, then, are really Satan and the other fallen angels. We seek justice in seeing them punished.

- In 2 Kings, we read that Ahab's successor Ahaziah turns to Baal-zebub, the god of Ekron, to know the future. As a result, Elijah tells him that he will die in his unfaithfulness.

- Azariah dies without a son, so his brother becomes king. There are now two kings named Jehoram, one in Israel and one in Judah.

- In 2 Chronicles 24, we again see Joash, who became king at age seven. He has a good mentor in the priest Jehoiada, who helps Joash be good and strong. Joash reinstates Temple worship, as well as the tax to ensure this worship.

- When Jehoiada dies, though, Joash stops being faithful to the Lord. When Jehoiada's son Zechariah tries to call Joash back to righteousness, he has him killed by stoning. This evil act causes Joash to be murdered by his own subjects.

- Joash could have died a hero, as a king who was faithful and led the people into righteousness and blessing. Instead, he dies a villain.

- Like Joash, we too can fail in our fidelity to the Lord. We need to discover mentors who will tell us when we are going the wrong way and draw us back to faithfulness. We need to pray to God for the grace to have our hearts and minds fully converted to him.

Take It to **Prayer**

Father in heaven, we give you praise, and we thank you. We thank you for your faithfulness, your faithful love, and the fact that, Lord, in your compassion you do not hide your face from us. There are so many times when in the midst of distress, in the midst of our brokenness, in the midst of failure on our part you remain present even when we cannot see you or feel you. We declare with faith that you are still there. Even when you are hidden, you are active. Even when we cannot see you, you are still present. And so we praise your name. We glorify you. We say, Lord, continue to be present. Continue to help us to cling to you when all else has failed and when everyone else has failed us. In Jesus' name we pray. Amen.

Dive **Deeper**

Who is that person in your life, like Jehoiada's son, who can point out when you're going the wrong way and call you back to faithfulness to the Lord? Thank God for this person, pray for him or her, and maybe send a message expressing gratitude for his or her role in your life!

Reflect on the **Word**

- Amaziah, king of Judah, goes into battle with three hundred thousand men of Judah and a hundred thousand hired men of Israel. When a prophet warns him not to fight with the hired men, Amaziah is faithful. The Lord provides the victory.

- But Amaziah's heart turns away from the Lord to the gods of Seir.

- Amaziah then challenges Israel to battle, but Israel soundly defeats Judah, seizing all the gold, silver, and vessels that are in the Temple. They also seize the treasuries of the king's house and take hostages.

- In 2 Kings 2, we see the transition from Elijah to Elisha. In the Bible, the eldest son inherits a double share of the father's property. Here, Elisha asks for a double portion of Elijah's spirit. So Elisha regards himself as the "son" of Elijah and therefore asks for his inheritance.

- Elijah replies that this will be done if Elisha sees him taken up to heaven. Elisha does see it as Elijah is taken up by fiery chariots.

- Elisha picks up Elijah's coat, and he then can do what Elijah did. For example, Elijah had placed his cloak upon the water of the Jordan, separating it in two. Now Elijah can do the same. Elijah raised someone from the dead; we will see Elisha do that and more, for he has double the portion of Elijah's spirit.

- Elisha returns to Bethel, where he is jeered at and shown no honor. Remember that Bethel is one of the places set up for worship instead of the Temple. This speaks to the battle between idolatry and worship of the true God.

- We must worship the Lord the way he commands to be worshipped. God is willing to fight for his people to show them the difference between true and false worship.

Take It to **Prayer**

Father in heaven, we give you praise, and we thank you. We thank you for the deliverance that you have given us. We thank you for delivering us from the hand of the Evil One. We thank you for all the times that you have helped us through dangers that we didn't even know about. Thank you, Lord. No matter what our age is on this day, day 171 of The Bible in a Year, whether we are still in our single digits in our years, or whether we are approaching triple digits in years, God, none of those days were earned by us. None of those days are things we deserve. Even this breath right now, even this heartbeat right now, we don't deserve. They are just simply your gift. And you have brought us to this day, and you give us this breath, and you continue to allow our hearts to beat in our chests, and we thank you. Please receive our thanks today. In Jesus' name. Amen.

Dive **Deeper**

God has given his people the extraordinary gift of the Mass, the sacred act of true worship. If possible, make time this week to go to an additional Mass at a parish near you to celebrate this act of true worship of the Lord.

Reflect on the **Word**

- In 2 Kings 3, we see an alliance between Jehoram, king of Israel; Jehoshaphat, king of Judah; and an unnamed king of Edom to go to war against Moab.

- When the three armies run out of water, Elisha performs a miracle.

- In the early morning, when the Moabites see the sun rising up over the water, they think it is blood and believe their enemies have killed each other. In the end, the three allied armies defeat Moab.

- In 2 Chronicles 26, we meet Uzziah, who becomes king at sixteen and reigns over Judah for fifty-two years. Uzziah is a good king at first, "but when he was strong he grew proud, to his destruction" (2 Chronicles 26:16).

- He goes into the sacred place to offer incense, though he is warned by the priest Azariah and the other priests not to do so. Uzziah wants to worship the way he wants rather than as the Lord commanded. As punishment, he contracts leprosy.

- We all need to be on guard against this way of thinking. After God blesses us, we can be tempted to decide to do things our own way.

- Uzziah's son Jotham becomes mighty because he walks in the way of the Lord. He will reign for sixteen years.

Take It to **Prayer**

Father in heaven, we do praise and bless your name, and may you be blessed above everyone, above all things. May you be honored and glorified. May you be worshipped and loved because you are love, Lord God, and you reveal your heart of love to us and your heart of love that is for us. In Jesus' name we pray. Amen.

Dive **Deeper**

What happened *when God's people divided into two separate kingdoms?*

One of the most destructive events in the Old Testament was the division of the united kingdom of David into two nations, Judah and Israel, in 930 BC. The kingdom established by David continued under his son Solomon, but it ended abruptly when Rehoboam, Solomon's son, refused to rule in a just and kind manner. As a result, the ten northern tribes broke away and formed a separate kingdom. In the south, the kingdom of Judah would maintain the royal line leading to Jesus.

The boundary between the two kingdoms was just north of the city of David, Jerusalem. This posed a significant challenge for Israel in the north as the people were now cut off from worship in the Temple. As a result, they developed new religious practices, establishing Bethel and Dan as new worship sites. It would not be long before their worship devolved into idolatry.

Worship in the southern kingdom of Judah continued in the Temple, and the Law of Moses remained the norm for religious and political life. While Israel and Judah were two distinct nations, there were occasions when they cooperated with each other to defeat a common enemy. We see this in 2 Kings 3, when Jehoshaphat in the south joined with Jehoram in the north to fight against Moab.

–Jeff Cavins

Reflect on the **Word**

- In 2 Chronicles we meet Ahaz, one of Judah's worst kings. Ahaz makes molten images for the Baals and even burns his sons as an offering in false worship. He foolishly leads the people into war, and Judah is defeated. Yet God is still fighting for his people.

- In 2 Kings 4, we read about the miracle of Elisha and the widow. This is similar to the miracle when Elijah multiplied the flour and oil for the widow of Zarephath and her son to save them from the famine. Elisha multiplies oil for a widow and her two sons and thus saves them.

- Also in 2 Kings 4 we hear of Elisha and the Shunammite couple. The woman has no children, but Elisha tells her that she will have a son by the same time next year.

- The woman is joyful because she has so longed for a child. Yet when he has grown, he falls ill and dies while working in a field with his father.

- Why would God bring her this child and then have him die? Why would God give such a blessing only to have it come to an end? We know that the Lord is God of the living and the dead—and everything that happens is for a larger purpose.

- In the case of the Shunammite woman, her son is restored to her. Ultimately, Jesus will reveal that death is not the end.

- Yet the death of loved ones causes us heartache. Let us pray for those whose hearts have been broken due to loss and have yet to be healed.

- If we know the end of the story, how we live the middle of the story will be dramatically changed. But we do know the end: Jesus has conquered death through his passion, death, and resurrection—and he will restore all things. He will make all things new.

Take It to **Prayer**

Father in heaven, we praise you, and we give you glory. We know that you are the one who accomplishes all that we do. In fact, we remember your words, the words of Jesus Christ, the only, beloved Son of God—the words of Jesus that are, "Without me, you can do nothing." So we ask that you please help us. Help us to remain as branches on the vine. Help us to remain not far from you but rooted so closely to you that we get all of our life, all of our power, all of our strength, all of our wisdom, all of our everything from you, that we can bear fruit—and fruit that will last, fruit that is for your glory and for the salvation of this world that you love and died for. So, God, please help us to never be separated from you. Help us to never be alienated from you. Help us to always be faithful. And when we are faithless, bring us back to you. In Jesus' name we pray. Amen.

Dive **Deeper**

Think of how you might lift up those who have suffered the loss of a loved one, particularly through miscarriage or the death of an infant. Offer up a prayer or sacrifice that they might be comforted in their sorrow. If you know someone who is grieving, make dinner for that person or send a message of love.

Reflect on the Word

- Naaman the Syrian is a brave general in the king of Syria's army. He has honor, reputation, wealth, and power, but he is a leper. He will die from his disease. Without God, success does not mean much.

- The course of Naaman's life is changed when a slave girl in his home brings news of Elisha's healings. Perhaps she knows the heart of God and wants to extend his healing even to those who are her enemies.

- Elisha tells Naaman to bathe in the Jordan River seven times. At first, he refuses because this cure seems too simple; he is looking for a spectacular sign.

- Here, we see a foreshadowing of the sacrament of Baptism. Like bathing seven times in the Jordan, being baptized seems "simple" in its action—but its power lies in the sacrifice of Jesus, and it transforms our lives.

- After he is healed, Naaman decides he will only worship the God of Israel, and he asks for two loads of earth so he can be standing on holy ground.

- Hosea is called to witness to the Lord in his words and actions. The Lord tells him to marry a prostitute, Gomer, knowing that she will be unfaithful. Hosea is called to be like the Lord because Gomer will be like the people of Israel—unfaithful, giving their hearts to others.

- In Hosea 2, the prophet entreats the people of Israel not to go after false lovers; any gifts they have received are from the Lord.

- Remember the book of Joshua, when the people of Israel entered the Promised Land and faced the battle of Ai and the Valley of Achor. A place of devastation is made a place of hope by the Lord. God can make our place of shame a victory—a place where we know how profoundly we are loved.

Take It to **Prayer**

Father in heaven, we give you praise, and we love you. We receive your love from you because you show yourself to be faithful when we are faithless. You show that you want us even when we are wanton. You show us, O God, that your love is unstoppable. Your love is unchangeable. It is not our beauty that draws you to us. It is your love that moves you to us. And so please continue to draw near. Continue to take us back when we stray. And continue to bar our way when we want to walk or run away. In Jesus' name we pray. Amen.

Dive **Deeper**

Hosea is called to witness to the Lord in his words and actions. While we are not called to the exact same way of life as Hosea, we *are* called to be faithful disciples of Jesus in prayer and in our everyday activities and interactions. Identify how you could better witness to the Lord in your words or actions today. Choose one way—and do it.

Reflect on the **Word**

- In 2 Kings 6 and 7, we see Elisha perform more miracles and receive insight and knowledge from the Lord.

- The king of Syria sends an army against the city in which Elisha and his servant are dwelling. Elisha says, "Fear not, for those who are with us are more than those who are with them" (2 Kings 6:16).

- The Lord opens the eyes of Elisha's servant, who then sees the horses and chariots of fire surrounding Elisha. God has been protecting them the whole time; here, he allows the young man to see that he is present.

- Even during the siege of Samaria and the horrors of war, God is present— fighting on behalf of the unfaithful king and people of Israel.

- When the prophet Hosea speaks to the people, the "knowledge" he shares is not mere information but intimacy with the Lord.

- In Hosea 4:6, we read, "My people are destroyed for lack of knowledge." They know the Ten Commandments and have heard the words of the prophets, so they are not without information. But they have not known the Lord in a life-changing way.

- We need to *know* the Lord. Our goal is to have an increasingly deeper knowledge of the One who created us, redeemed us, and loves us.

Take It to **Prayer**

Father in heaven, we give you praise and we give you thanks because it is true. Your mercy is towards those who fear you. As far as the east is from the west, so far do you remove our transgressions from us, Lord God. Your mercy is limitless. It is unstoppable. It is infinite. Your mercy is given to us the most when we need it the most and deserve it the least. And that is what your love is like. And so, thank you so much. You know our frame. You remember that we are dust. You know how feeble we can be. You know how weak we can be. You know what causes us to sin, and yet you still give us your grace so that your life may abound in us. So help us. Help us to say yes to you this day and every day. In Jesus' name we pray. Amen.

Dive **Deeper**

"Knowing God" means much more than knowing *about* him. It is having a relationship with him, which requires a consistent, focused prayer life. Today, reflect on how you pray. What are some ways you can make your prayer deeper and more consistent?

Reflect on the **Word**

- 2 Kings 8 refers to the story of Elisha and the Shunammite woman. We also see a restatement of many of the stories we have already seen.

- In Hosea, we see a repeated theme: God has given his people everything they could possibly want, yet they have taken his blessings and offered them to idols.

- Hosea begs the people of Israel to turn away from their evil ways. Though God's faithfulness is unending, the time for repentance is finite. Hosea reminds the people of Israel that God loves them, but if they choose something other than the Lord, he will let them go to what they have chosen.

- In the Sermon on the Mount, Jesus says that a person who listens to his words and does not act on them will be like one who builds his house upon sand (see Matthew 7:24-27).

- As we build our lives, we need to ask, "Are we building upon ourselves? Are we building on the false gods of the world? Or are we building on the Lord Jesus?"

- We build our lives on the Lord when we follow his will, obey his commandments, repent of our sins, and turn to him.

- Anyone who truly loves God wants to spend eternity with him. But it is our choice. If we choose something other than him, we will get what we have chosen.

Take It to **Prayer**

Father in heaven, thank you so much. Thank you for the gift of yourself and the gift of your Son. Thank you for fighting for us. Vain is the help of the people around us. While we need each other and while we need to lift each other up and fight for one another, with you we shall do bravely. With you we shall do valiantly. And it is you who accomplish all we have done. And it is you who will tread down our foes. Help us to be faithful to you and to be faithful in waiting on you and to be faithful to allow you to show up and to fight for us as you want to fight for us, not as we want to be fought for. Because, Lord, your will surpasses our best-laid plans. Your wisdom surpasses our depth of understanding as the ocean surpasses a puddle, Lord God. So we just praise you, and we trust you today. In Jesus' name. Amen.

Dive **Deeper**

How can we keep track *of everything that is going on in 2 Kings?*

First, keep in mind that you are reading a compilation of the actions of kings from two distinct kingdoms—Israel in the north and Judah in the south. (Unfortunately, most of these kings end up turning away from the Lord.) This narrative sets the background for Jesus' descent from the line of Judah. Second, pay attention to where each king is from. For example, the kings in the north are referred to as the king of Samaria, Israel, or Ephraim. Likewise, kings from the south may be said to be from Judah or Jerusalem.

Third, use *The Great Adventure Catholic Bible* and *The Bible Timeline®* Chart (both published by Ascension) to see who the prophets are and to whom they are speaking. Make notes in the margin of your Bible to keep track. This will help you understand the unique messages of God to Israel and Judah. Finally, you may want to use markers to highlight the various kings, using different colors for Israel and Judah.

–Jeff Cavins

Reflect on the **Word**

- Psalm 109 follows the story of David. He had enemies who sought his life, as well as those he thought were friends but who were not.

- David wants his enemies to receive the Lord's justice. Before we can forgive, we need to know that something unjust needs to be forgiven.

- Jesus prayed, "Father, forgive them; for they know not what they do" (Luke 23:34), even as he allowed his freedom, life, and dignity to be stripped away during his passion and death.

- 2 Kings 9 presents the death of Jezebel in detail. Jehu is anointed to be the next king of Israel, so Jezebel attempts to seduce Jehu and prevent him from overturning the current dynasty. She does not realize that her servants will turn against her.

- We see Jezebel and Ahab being justly punished for the evil they have been doing for so long.

- A theme through the Bible is that the Lord allows us to choose—and receive the fruits of what we have chosen. This is a key concept in Hosea. In the end, the people of Israel get what they have chosen—exile.

- Hosea pleads for the people to repent: "Return, O Israel, to the LORD your God, for you have stumbled because of your iniquity. Take with you words and return to the LORD" (Hosea 14:1-2). The Lord promises, "I will heal their faithlessness; I will love them freely" (Hosea 14:4). This is a powerful word of promise, but it is one that goes unheeded.

- But the story is not over. At a certain point in history, God himself becomes one of us—and he extends his blessing to all the tribes, peoples, and nations of the world through Christ.

Take It to **Prayer**

Father in heaven, we give you praise, and we pray for your grace. We pray for your help. We come before you in prayer and in fasting. We come before you in our need because just like David in this Psalm 109, God, we have those who stand against us. We have those who curse us, those who have kept the blessing far from them. Unlike David who asks for those who have cursed him to experience curses themselves, we ask for the grace to be able to call out injustice when we see it, to name evil when we see it, but also a willingness to be like Christ, to be able to extend mercy, to be able to extend forgiveness. So Lord God, unlike David, we do not ask for curses to come upon our enemies. We ask for their conversion. We ask for you to love them into a new life. We ask for you to give them the blessings that will change their hearts so that they know who you are and that they will follow you with their entire lives. In Jesus' name we pray for our enemies. We pray for those who love us. We pray for those who do not love us as they should. And we pray for each other. Amen.

Dive **Deeper**

ANCIENT PORTRAYAL
OF AN ISRAELITE KING

This black limestone obelisk honoring King Shalmaneser III, circa 825 BC, is displayed in the British Museum in London. The inscription identifies one figure as Jehu, son of Omri, an Israelite king. (See 2 Kings 9.)

Illustration and
caption from Ritmeyer
Archaeological Design

Reflect on the **Word**

- When Jehu asks the people which of Ahab's seventy sons they want to be their king, they instead choose him. So Jehu commands them to kill all of Ahab's sons and bring him their heads. He does this to eliminate any threat to his rule from the house of Ahab.

- Later in chapter 10, Jehu eliminates the false worship of Baal by killing its followers. He did not fully restore true worship of the Lord, however, because he keeps Jeroboam's golden calves in Bethel and Dan.

- The prophet Amos prophesies several decades after these events, when Jeroboam II is the king of Israel.

- Amos frequently uses the expression "For three transgressions and for four," which indicates the adding of sin upon sin. He says that there will be consequences.

- In Amos 2, we read about the transgressions of Judah: they have rejected the Law of the Lord and continue in their false worship, even though they have the Temple. Amos calls them back to true worship of the Lord.

- He then speaks out against Israel for both false worship and injustice in the sight of the Lord. The people of Israel are not caring for the poor and the helpless.

- Though the Lord continues to bless his people with prosperity, they willfully continue turning away from him. His judgment becomes unavoidable.

- The constant refrain of the prophets is this: *Return to the Lord before it is too late.* Now is the time for all of us to turn back to God and allow him to make us whole.

Take It to **Prayer**

Father in heaven, we give you praise. Lord, thank you for your Word. Thank you for calling us back to yourself. Thank you for the voices and the words of the prophets that you inspire by your Holy Spirit to call the people of Israel, the people of Judah, and the people of all the nations back to your heart. Lord God, you call us back too. Help us to hear the words of the prophet Amos and all the words of your Scriptures that call us back, that are your logic of love—that you give us so much and you expect so much from us. You expect us to be faithful to you when you are so faithful to us. You expect us to love you in return when you have given us so much love. Lord God, help us to repent to you before it is too late. Help us to turn to you with our whole heart, mind, soul, and strength. Help us to love you with everything we are and everything we have. In Jesus' name we pray. Amen.

Dive **Deeper**

Today, reflect on the consistent call of the prophets: *Return to the Lord before it is too late*. Sometimes, returning to the Lord requires a dramatic conversion. Often, though, it means simply surrendering to God's plan and seeking to deepen your relationship with him every day through prayer.

Reflect on the **Word**

- In 2 Kings 11, we again see the story of Athaliah. Reigning over Judah, she kills all of the descendants of Ahaziah except for Joash, also called Jehoash.

- The prophet Amos calls the people higher. This is the role of a prophet—to speak the truth of the Lord to those who need to hear it.

- Amos proclaims that the Lord takes no delight in the people's solemn assemblies because they are not taking care of the poor.

- We read, "Woe to those who are at ease in Zion, and to those who feel secure on the mountain of Samaria ... Woe to those who lie upon beds of ivory, and stretch themselves upon their couches ... who drink wine in bowls, and anoint themselves with the finest oils" (Amos 6:1, 4, 6).

- Many today live in similar indulgence and extravagance. In our comfort, we can often neglect the needs of the poor and fail to see the injustice around us.

- Even if we do not live in an extravagant way, where is God calling us to serve those in need better?

- As St. Teresa of Calcutta said, "If we have no peace, it is because we have forgotten that we belong to each other."*

- Time is short, and eternity is long. So we need to turn back to the Lord while we still have time.

---

* Mother Teresa, *Where There Is Love, There Is God: A Path to Closer Union with God and Greater Love for Others*, ed. Brian Kolodiejchuk, MC (New York: Doubleday, 2010), 330, books.google.com.

Take It to **Prayer**

Father in heaven, thank you. Thank you so much for your Word. Thank you for revealing your heart to us. Please receive our praise. As we pray Psalm 122, we ask that you please receive this song of praise, that we are glad when they said to us, let us go to the house of the Lord. And yes, of course we know that the Temple, the house of the Lord in Jerusalem, no longer stands. And yet, Lord God, you have made all those who are baptized temples of your Holy Spirit. You have given us these churches. You continue to abide and dwell in tabernacles throughout the world. We ask you to please help us to always value your presence. Help us to always seek out your face and help us to always do your will in everything. In Jesus' name we pray. Amen.

Dive **Deeper**

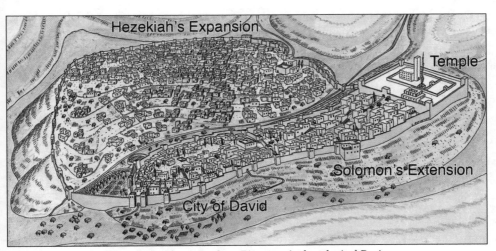

Illustration and caption from Ritmeyer Archaeological Design

JERUSALEM IN THE TIME OF HEZEKIAH

In this drawing, we see how Jerusalem developed after the days of Solomon. King Hezekiah built a new city wall around this hill to protect it from invasion. (See 2 Chronicles 29–32.)

Reflect on the **Word**

- Amos speaks to Israel, telling them that they will have destruction rather than grace and mercy because they have abandoned the ways of the Lord.

- We hear that the people deal deceitfully and unjustly, both with each other and with God: they "trample upon the needy, and bring the poor of the land to an end" (Amos 8:4).

- The people ask when the Sabbath will be over so that they may again sell grain. They observe the letter of the law in keeping the Sabbath, but they long to return to business as usual.

- Do we long for the things of God to be over so that we can move on to our own pursuits? Where are our hearts? We need to let our hearts be changed, just as the people of Israel needed a change of heart.

- Because the people of Israel refuse to change, the Lord allows them to be destroyed by the Assyrians.

- Destruction and captivity are not the final words, however. The final word is *restoration*. The Lord promises, "I will restore the fortunes of my people Israel, and they shall rebuild the ruined cities and inhabit them" (Amos 9:14).

- This promise is fulfilled in Jesus. We thank God for restoring us, for calling us back—this day and every day.

Take It to **Prayer**

Father in heaven, we give you praise. We thank you so much. If it had not been for you, the psalmist David says in the "psalm of ascent" here, if it had not been for you then we would have died in our affliction. If it had not been for you, Lord God, we would have perished long ago—if it had not been for you and what you have done. But Lord God, you have helped us escape. You have helped us to this day, and we ask you to continue. Continue to help us be yours this day and every day of our lives. In Jesus' name. Amen.

Dive **Deeper**

Why couldn't any of the kings—even the good ones—get rid of the high places used for worshipping false gods?

At first glance, we might think that it would be a simple matter for a king to order the destruction of the places of false worship. But here we come face-to-face with the complexities of our fallen human nature. The Lord commanded his kings to rid the land of false worship, but concupiscence—the tendency to sin and self-centeredness—clouded their judgment. In other words, like all of us, kings could be weak when they relied on their own strength rather than the strength of God.

Power grabs, concerns about reputation, and the lure of a perceived better life drew many kings' hearts away from God into what appeared to be "greener pastures." The psalmist reminds us, "The fool says in his heart, 'There is no God'" (Psalm 14:1). In many ways, for those who believe in God, this becomes, "No, God!" When a king failed to seek God's wisdom or listen to the counsel of prophets the Lord sent, he could begin to follow the whims of his own heart—which could lead to disaster for his nation. A king was victorious only when he learned that we do not live by bread alone but by everything that proceeds out of the mouth of the Lord (see Deuteronomy 8:3).

–Jeff Cavins

Reflect on the **Word**

- In 2 Kings 15, we see that chaos reigns in the kingdom of Israel, with murders, intrigue, and a series of kings.

- The Assyrians invade Israel and carry people into exile. Thus begins the destruction of the Northern Kingdom.

- We are introduced to the prophet Jonah, who prophesies to Jeroboam II, an evil king of Israel (see 2 Kings 14:25).

- God tells Jonah to go to Nineveh in Assyria and call its people to repentance, but Jonah refuses, running away to Tarshish. The Assyrians are the enemies of the Israelites, and Jonah does not want the people of Nineveh to repent and experience God's mercy. Instead, he wants them to suffer for their sins.

- In calling even the enemies of his people to repentance, the Lord demonstrates his kindness and mercy.

- Jonah is upset when the Lord spares Nineveh from destruction and is also upset when the plant that shaded him dies. The Lord inquires why Jonah has more pity for a plant than for the people of Nineveh. In this, God shows the depth of his love.

- We, too, can speak God's words and still have hardened hearts when we refuse to extend his mercy to others. We should seek to be more like Amos than Jonah. We are called to speak and live the truth in a way that makes our lives a testimony to Jesus.

Take It to **Prayer**

Father in heaven, we give you praise and thank you so much. Lord, you do see us and you observe us, you watch us—and not just watch us to "bust" us. Lord God, you don't just watch us to catch us doing something wrong. You are attentive to us. You attend to us, which makes no sense, Lord God, because you are the God of the universe. And yet, these people—us—that you have made in your image and likeness ... you attend to us with the love of a Father, because you have made us your sons and your daughters. And so we thank you. And we know that you hear every one of our prayers. We know that you know all of our needs. And so in this moment we bring our hearts to you, God. Not just my words here, but the words, the heart, the needs, the desires of every person listening to these words, Lord God. I know that you know us. You know us by name. And every person who is listening to these words with a desire in their heart, with grief in their heart, with hope or joy or love in their heart, every person listening to these words, Lord God ... you know the secret of the heart. And you are the answer. You are the answer to the questions of our hearts, to the grief of our hearts, to the brokenness of our hearts. You are the answer. And so we praise you and we pray to you and we love you. May you be glorified, Lord God. In Jesus' name. Amen.

Dive **Deeper**

***Is the story** of Jonah historical?*

When called by God to preach to Nineveh, Jonah cannot stomach the task of speaking to his ancestral enemy about God's merciful love. He flees on a ship and almost drowns, but God rescues Jonah by sending a large fish to swallow him. Jonah goes on to proclaim God's Word to Nineveh.

While many modern biblical scholars see the book of Jonah as an allegory, a story, rather than a recounting of actual historical events, the Church takes no definitive position on this matter. So Catholics are free to read Jonah either as historical or as a story of how God deals mercifully with everyone, even those who were enemies of his people.

–Jeff Cavins

Reflect on the **Word**

- In 2 Kings 16, we read that Ahaz does not live like his father Jotham or his grandfather Uzziah. Instead, he turns away from the worship of the Lord to idolatry. He even sacrifices his own son.

- After meeting the king of Assyria, Ahaz tells Uriah the priest that he wants an altar built just like the pagan altar he sees on his visit. Ahaz will act as a priest, offering false sacrifices on a false altar.

- Syria and Israel join forces against Judah. The prophet Isaiah tells Ahaz to ask the Lord for a sign, but Ahaz responds that he will not tempt the Lord (see Isaiah 7:10-12). He does not say this because he is humble but because he already has a plan of his own—to make a deal with the king of Assyria rather than trusting in the Lord.

- Assyria will destroy Israel and lead the people into exile. Eventually Judah will be destroyed, as well.

- During Isaiah's time, Micah is also serving God as a prophet. Like the other prophets, he proclaims both judgment and hope—God's judgment if the people remain far from the Lord, but hope if they draw near to him.

- Assyria and Babylon will destroy the kingdoms of Israel and Judah because the leaders are corrupt.

- In the midst of the word of judgment, we see a promise of restoration after exile: "The mountain of the house of the LORD shall be established as the highest of the mountains, and shall be raised up above the hills; and peoples shall flow to it" (Micah 4:1). Ultimately, Jesus fulfills this promise. In the New Covenant, he extends the blessings of God to the people of Israel and to the entire world through the Church.

- Remember God's threefold promise to Abraham—kingdom, land, and worldwide blessing. Micah affirms that this blessing will happen after exile, and that the Lord himself will judge the nations.

Take It to **Prayer**

Father in heaven, we give you praise. God, thank you so much. Thank you. You are—I love the title of this psalm—the inescapable God. You are the inescapable God because you formed us in the depths of our being. You formed us when we were hidden in our mothers' wombs. You, Lord God, have known us. And you have known us through and through, known us thoroughly. And we can never escape you. And why would we, Lord God? Help us to let you find us. Help us to seek after you and not run from you and not race to the ends of the sea or to fly to earth. And we ask you to please help us to stop, to turn back to you, and to be found by you because you are the God who loves us. And help us to let ourselves be loved by you, in this unstoppable and inescapable way. We make this prayer in Jesus' name. Amen.

Dive **Deeper**

Trust in the Lord is difficult, especially because we often prefer our own plans and security to those of God. Surrender your plans to the Lord today and offer him any situations that are particularly difficult to hand over. Pray the words "Jesus, I trust in you" from your heart.

Reflect on the **Word**

- 2 Kings 17 presents the fall of the northern kingdom of Israel, when the ten tribes are exiled by the Assyrians.

- This is a critical moment—these tribes are now gone, leaving just the two tribes in the south, Judah and Benjamin. Eventually, Judah and Benjamin will be exiled into Babylon, as well, but they will return and resettle the land.

- John 4 recounts how Jesus meets the Samaritan woman at the well. We read that Samaritans have nothing to do with Jews. Here in 2 Kings 17, we see the foundation of the tension between the Jews and the Samaritans. The king of Assyria exiles the Jews from Samaria and brings in people of five foreign nations to settle the cities of Samaria.

- In Micah 5, we hear the prophecy of Jesus' birth in Bethlehem: "But you, O Bethlehem Ephrathah ... from you shall come forth for me one who is to be ruler in Israel" (Micah 5:2). Micah is telling the people that they will be scattered but from Bethlehem in Judah will come a ruler who will bring them back.

- The question is asked in Micah 6, "With what shall I come before the LORD, and bow myself before God on high?" Micah replies: "He has showed you, O man, what is good; and what does the LORD require of you but to do justice, and to love kindness, and to walk humbly with your God?" (Micah 6:6, 8).

Take It to **Prayer**

Father in heaven, thank you. Thank you for your Word. Thank you for your love for us. Thank you for calling us back to you. Lord God, the psalmist David is praying. He is praying to you for help because yes, it's true that we face the snares of our enemies. We face the net that our enemies have laid for us, and now those could be human enemies, but just like St. Paul said, the real enemies we face are not flesh and blood, but are principalities and powers, the evil spirits, Satan, that roams around the world seeking the ruin of souls. And so we pray for your protection against the true enemy. Lord God, you have revealed to us that the forces that are against us are the world, the flesh, and the devil. The fallen world. The corrupt world. Our own fallen flesh. And the fallen angel of Satan. All three of those obstacles, all three of those enemies trip us up. They become snares for us. And so we just ask you, help us not only to be vigilant and to be wise, to be able to have our eyes open clearly and to see those traps of the world, the flesh, and the devil—but also, to have the courage in the midst of the battle to call out to you, in the midst of the battle to actually fight. Lord God, let us never, ever just exchange comfort for truth. Let us never try to escape discomfort by capitulating to the traps and the snares of the enemy. Help us always to be courageous, to be wise, and to be yours in all things. In Jesus' name we pray. Amen.

Dive **Deeper**

Pray, worship, and adore the Lord today, in Mass and Eucharistic Adoration, if possible. Spend time with him on earth so that your heart will be prepared for eternity with him in heaven.

Divided Kingdom **Recap**

As we entered the Divided Kingdom period, it appeared that the Davidic dynasty was falling apart. Geographic boundaries had changed, leaders had lost the trust of the people, and the liturgical norms had been compromised. The influence of pagan neighbors with their foreign gods increased the temptation toward idolatry for Israel and Judah. Both kingdoms succeeded and failed as one, and the prophets cried out for justice and renewed holiness. Ultimately, the period ended in the Exile.

Divided Kingdom **Review Questions**

Use these questions to test your knowledge of the time period you just finished. Answers are below. No matter how many you can answer, celebrate the accomplishment of finishing another period!

1. When Jeroboam, the leader of the northern tribes, asked Rehoboam how he was going to rule, whom was he afraid Rehoboam would emulate?

2. From which kingdom would the Messiah come?

3. Who are the two prophets who spoke to the northern kingdom of Israel?

4. Who was the courageous prophet who defeated the prophets of Baal?

5. Which king of Judah had the longest reign and was one of the most evil kings?

6. Which king of Judah, mentioned in the genealogy of Jesus, was considered one of the most righteous kings of Judah?

7. While 1 and 2 Chronicles revisit many of the events recounted in the two books of Kings, which kingdom do the books of Chronicles focus on?

7. Judah
6. Hezekiah
5. Manasseh
4. Elijah
3. Hosea and Amos
2. Judah
1. Solomon

Baby blue is the color of the **EXILE** time period because it symbolizes Judah "singing the blues" in Babylon.

Key **Events & Figures**

The period of the Exile is one of the saddest chapters in Israel's history. Both Israel in the north and Judah in the south were declining in faithfulness to the Lord and drifting further away from their unique calling among the nations. God sent numerous prophets to point out their waywardness and call them to return to the Lord—or face the consequences. Selfish kings combined with the lure of foreign gods resulted in both kingdoms adopting the ways of the world around them rather than being faithful to the ways of God.

The Lord uses two great nations to discipline his people for their infidelity to him: Assyria and Babylon. In 722 BC, the Assyrians destroy the ten tribes of Israel and take many into exile, bringing in peoples from five other regions to live in the land. Likewise, God uses Nebuchadnezzar, king of Babylon, to conquer Judah and ultimately destroy Jerusalem and the Temple in 587 BC. The exiles will spend the next seventy years in Babylon.

What **Changes?**

The period of the Exile is one of great change for God's people. The changes that take place are social, religious, and geographic. Because of their infidelity, God allows their enemies to conquer the Chosen People and end life as they know it. Their time of reckoning has come. For some, exile simply continues their broken relationship with God; for others, though, exile brings healing and restoration.

The ten tribes of Israel, as they existed in the Divided Kingdom, will be permanently lost. Judah, though, will make a new home in Babylon, thinking, praying, and yearning for seventy years.

Reflect on the **Word**

- Psalm 141 is a great prayer to begin the day: "Set a guard over my mouth, O Lord, keep watch over the door of my lips" (Psalm 141:3).

- In 2 Kings and 2 Chronicles, we see the story of Hezekiah. His father was Ahaz, one of the worst kings of Judah, but Hezekiah is one of the best kings. Our history is not our destiny. Our ancestors do not determine our future. While Hezekiah does not condemn Ahaz in these chapters of 2 Kings or 2 Chronicles, his actions undo all of his father's bad actions.

- Some of the good kings reestablished Temple worship, but they were unwilling to remove the idolatrous places throughout the land. Of course, this did not lead the people to holiness. Hezekiah understands his responsibility as king. He not only reinstates true worship in the Temple but also removes idols from the land.

- In 2 Kings 18, we see that the ambassador (the *Rabshakeh*) from the king of Assyria, Sennacherib, comes to give a message to Hezekiah. When asked to speak in Aramaic so that the people will not understand and be discouraged, the Rabshakeh refuses—he wants everyone to hear and believe that it is Hezekiah's unwillingness to give in to Sennacherib that will cause them to suffer.

- The Rabshakeh explains that Assyria conquered many other lands and their gods did not protect them. It would be foolish to think the Lord will protect Israel, he says.

- In 2 Kings 19 and the chapters that follow, an important question is considered: Is it worth relying on the Lord rather than making an alliance with one's enemy?

- In the end, Hezekiah not only purifies Temple worship, he also relies upon God in the face of opposition and danger.

- Here we learn a valuable lesson: We must worship God in the way he commands, and then we place our trust in him, especially in difficult situations.

Take It to **Prayer**

Father in heaven, we thank you so much. Thank you for your Word and your kindness. Thank you so much for the fact that you receive our prayers and that for whatever reason, God, our prayers matter to you. Our hearts matter to you. Our lives matter to you. The hairs on our head ... apparently, for whatever reason, God—this doesn't make any sense, but we matter to you. Thank you. Thank you for hearing our prayers. Thank you for the fact that when we listen to your Word, that that matters to you. That it honors you. That it gives you glory and that you receive it. Receive this time that we have spent together, this time that we have spent listening to your Word as our gift to you. When we know truly what it is, it is your gift to us. You are so good, God. We thank you and praise your name. We ask you to keep us. Help us to remain faithful, and if we haven't been faithful, make us so. In Jesus' name we pray. Amen.

Serpent in the Wilderness, Julius Schnorr von Carolsfeld

Dive **Deeper**

THE BRONZE SERPENT

This image shows the bronze serpent God commanded Moses to construct. (See Numbers 21.) By the time of the events of 2 Kings 18, however, the people were worshipping it. Consequently, King Hezekiah broke it into pieces.

Reflect on the **Word**

- 2 Kings 19 and 2 Chronicles 30 highlight that Hezekiah, though not a perfect king, is one of the best.

- Sennacherib says that Assyria has destroyed many nations, whose gods did not save them, so Hezekiah should not think his people will be saved by the Lord. Hezekiah takes Sennacherib's letter mocking his trust in the Lord, reads it, and spreads it before the Lord.

- Hezekiah knows the battle is impossible to win and acknowledges that only God can save the day.

- Like Hezekiah, we need to turn to God in difficult, even seemingly impossible, times.

- In 2 Chronicles 30, we see that Hezekiah reinstitutes the feast of Passover so that the Lord will be worshipped in the way he has commanded.

- Hezekiah sends word to the remnant tribes in the north and invites them back to Temple worship. God's people are not meant to be divided but to be one nation that blesses him—and is blessed by him.

- Certain moments call for extended celebration, such as this one, when Hezekiah reinstitutes the feast of Passover.

- Let us reflect on the ways the Lord is calling us to give him our whole hearts—by eliminating the idols in our lives and worshipping him as he has asked us to worship him.

Take It to **Prayer**

Father in heaven, we thank you and give you praise. Just like David here is praying for deliverance from enemies, we have been praying these last days for deliverance from persecution, from evil, and from obstacles, from enemies. Because we know that you are the God who hears our prayers. And so there is no obstacle, there is no enemy, there is no difficulty, there is no persecutor or persecution that is bigger than you, is stronger than you. You are the Lord God of all. And so we trust in you this day and every day. We trust you with our hopes. We trust you with our dreams. We trust you with our fears. We trust you with those that we love, Lord God. We place them into your hands. With all the things we love, we place them into your hands. With our very selves, we place ourselves into your hands. Please receive us as your children this day and every day into eternity. In Jesus' name we pray. Amen.

Dive **Deeper**

Today, prayerfully reflect on the following questions:
In what ways is the Lord calling me to give him my whole heart in worship? How can I get rid of the idols in my life and love God more fully?

Reflect on the **Word**

- In 2 Kings 20, we read that Hezekiah is near death. Though Isaiah tells him he will not recover, Hezekiah beseeches the Lord and receives a miraculous healing. He lives for another fifteen years.

- An envoy from Babylon arrives. Seeking to impress him, Hezekiah foolishly shows the envoy all his treasures and weapons.

- In response, Isaiah rebukes Hezekiah for revealing the kingdom's secrets to a nation that will one day invade and destroy and exile the people.

- Hezekiah shows a certain shallowness of character by being pleased because Judah will not fall to Babylon during his reign. These are not the words of a king who takes care of his people and honors the Lord.

- We should never put our trust in rulers. No matter how good a king, president, or governor—or even a priest or friend—might be, he or she remains a fallen, broken human being who can sin.

- At the end of his life, Hezekiah thinks of himself. Yet he was a good king who reinstituted proper worship in the Temple, thus encouraging the people to praise and give glory to the Lord. He considered the needs of both present and future generations.

Take It to **Prayer**

Father in heaven, we thank you and give you praise. Happy the people whose God is the Lord. You are our God, and we are blessed because you are good. We thank you for your goodness, Lord God, today. Whether we are praying these words, hearing these words early in the morning, in the middle of our day, at the end of our day, whatever time we are, we are blessed just to know you, God. We are blessed just to have you in our lives, to not go through this life not knowing who you are, not knowing who we are, not knowing where we come from or who we come from, not knowing who we are made for. We are made for you, Lord God. We give you praise and thank you. In Jesus' name we pray. Amen.

Dive **Deeper**

Pray this day for those who will take this journey through the Bible after you. They will be strengthened by your prayers!

Reflect on the **Word**

- In 2 Kings 21, we see that Manasseh is only twelve when he becomes king and that he will reign for fifty-five years.

- Unlike his father, Hezekiah, Manasseh does evil in the sight of the Lord and is one of the worst kings. Thus, he is like his grandfather Ahaz.

- Manasseh rebuilds the idols and pagan temples Hezekiah had destroyed and brings abominable things into the Temple. Here begins the downward spiral of the people of Israel where they again turn their backs to the Lord.

- We have heard from the prophets Amos, Micah, and Jonah. Now that we know more about Assyria's destruction of Israel, we can understand why Jonah was so reluctant to obey the Lord's command to go to Nineveh, in Assyria, and tell them to repent.

- Recall that Hezekiah prays for healing, and the Lord grants him an additional fifteen years of life. During this period, the Babylonian envoys visit, and Hezekiah brags to them of his riches; he is content that there will be peace and security in *his* days.

- St. Dominic Savio, who died at age fourteen, is known for preferring death rather than mortal sin. Hezekiah pleads with the Lord for a longer life, but he does not use those extra years to become a better person. Though he is a great king overall, Hezekiah becomes prideful in his last years.

- For those of us who are ill or have wounds of body, heart, or mind, we should pray for healing—both for ourselves and others who are suffering. And we should pray that any healing we experience leads us to become closer to the Lord.

- Let us use the time we have to be more like Jesus, to become the saints God has called us to be and redeemed us to be—to become an image of Jesus in the world.

Take It to **Prayer**

Father in heaven, we thank you so much. Lord, I ask you please this day, on day 187, I just ask you please to receive our praise once again because we can never tire of praising you, blessing you, giving glory to your holy name. So, Lord God, please receive our praise. Receive our thanks today. Help us to use our lives well. Help us to use whatever time you give us in this life well and wisely. Lord God, let not one of our days not help to make us better people, more faithful to you, more repentant of our sins, and more virtuous in your grace and your power and your strength. In Jesus' name we pray. Amen.

Dive **Deeper**

What is the remnant?

When the word "remnant" is used in the Bible, it refers to a small number of people who remain, usually in the wake of a devastating event. In the Old Testament, it is used for those who remained in the Promised Land after its conquest.

In 930 BC the united kingdom David established was divided. Eventually, due to their infidelity to the Lord, both kingdoms would be conquered and exiled by foreign nations. In 722 BC, the Assyrians destroyed the Northern Kingdom of Israel, carrying away many of the people to other countries. A small number—a remnant—was left behind, who would struggle to survive and continue to practice their faith. Then, in 587 BC, the Babylonians destroyed Jerusalem and took the educated and useful from Judah to Babylon. The remnant faced a unique set of challenges as the Temple, and its sacrificial system, had been destroyed.

During this period, the many prophets spoke to the people of the coming calamities—conquest, destruction, and exile—due to their unfaithfulness to the Lord. They also promised that the Lord would be merciful and one day return the exiles to their land.

–Jeff Cavins

Reflect on the **Word**

- The author of Proverbs frequently uses imagery to present various truths. Here, we see the image of an adulteress or harlot. Like all sin that calls to our hearts, adultery in the Bible is often a metaphor for idolatry. We saw this in Hosea, with his unfaithful wife, Gomer. It is an often-used image of the people of Israel being unfaithful to the Lord.

- The young man in Proverbs goes into the darkness so no one can see his sin. How many sins would we avoid if we were being observed?

- We seek to hide the dark, broken parts of our lives—even from ourselves. We can walk in the light by being accountable for our actions. We should seek to live in the light rather than darkness.

- 2 Chronicles 33 describes the actions of Manasseh, who sets up his own altars in the Temple and his own high places around Judah. Yet he is humbled when he is exiled to Babylon. He then repents of his sins, and the Lord hears his prayer.

- Remember that Josiah becomes king when he is only eight, and after eighteen years, Hilkiah, the high priest, finds the "lost" book of the Law in the Temple.

- Deuteronomy 17 states that each king was to have a personal copy of the Law, and he was to read it frequently. Similarly, Deuteronomy 31 tells us that the entire Law was to be read at an assembly of the tribes every seven years on the Feast of Tabernacles to keep the Law before the people.

- The book of the Law is a reminder of who the Lord is and the covenant he made with Israel, but somehow, it is lost. How many times has God revealed himself—and given himself—to us, and we set him aside and "lose" him?

Take It to **Prayer**

Father in heaven, we thank you, and we give you praise. Thank you for being such a good Dad to us, for loving us in our weakness. For loving us not only when we don't love you back, when we don't love each other, when we don't love the people that you have placed in our lives. Lord God, you still are love, and you still have made us for love, and you still call us to love, even when we have wandered away from you. Lord, you continue to call us back to you. Reveal your heart to us. Continue to reveal your Word to us this day and every day. Continue to allow us to hear your voice, to not just hear your voice, but to truly listen to the depths of your heart. In Jesus' name we pray. Amen.

Dive **Deeper**

ANCIENT SIGNET RING

This ancient ring bears the seal of Hanan, the son of the high priest Hilkiah. Hilkiah served at the time of King Josiah and was famous for finding a lost copy of the book of the Law. (See 2 Kings 22.)

Reflect on the **Word**

- In the books of Samuel, Kings, and Chronicles, we have the stories of leaders and of the "important people" in the king's house. But there are also the other people who live in those times, and they are all called to be faithful, regardless of what the kings do.

- It is easy to become preoccupied with the powerful in our world and claim that things are the worst or the best due to who is in charge. But we have to be responsible for ourselves and our own house regardless of where or when we are living. In Joshua's words, "But as for me and my house, we will serve the LORD" (Joshua 24:15).

- Josiah is a leader who brings about the people's conversion because he allows himself to be converted. As the Bible tells us, he follows the Lord with all his heart and soul.

- Regardless of what our families, friends, and neighbors or the rest of the nation are doing, we are called to follow the Lord, to love him with our hearts and souls.

- Though the people repent, there are still consequences. As 2 Kings 23:26 states, "Still the LORD did not turn from the fierceness of his great wrath."

- Destruction and exile will follow, as we will see in the next chapters. Nebuchadnezzar, king of Babylon, will conquer the holy city of Jerusalem, destroy the Temple, and send many into exile.

Take It to **Prayer**

Father, we thank you. Thank you for your gift. Thank you for who you are. Thank you for also continually revealing your heart to us, revealing your wisdom. Lord, as we journey through Proverbs, we ask that you please increase our wisdom. Increase our ability to see what is right and what is true. And not only to see it, not only to hear it, as we prayed yesterday, but to truly understand, to truly listen, to be able to truly hear in the depths of our mind and in our hearts that we can be wise—not just know a lot of stuff, but that we can be wise people in this world. Help us to be wise, so that we can wisely follow after you and wisely live and wisely lead the people who are under us, people that we are responsible for, our families, and our friends, and the people in our world. In Jesus' name we pray. Amen.

Dive **Deeper**

Dwell on the words of Joshua 24:15 in prayer.
In what ways does your house serve the Lord
faithfully? In what ways is there room for growth?

Reflect on the **Word**

- As we continue in Proverbs, we keep coming back to the wisdom of God.

- The foolish are always disconnected from God, whereas the wise see and value things correctly; they are able to hear the voice of the Lord.

- In 2 Chronicles 35, we see how Josiah shows his wisdom by reestablishing true worship and celebrating the Passover feast.

- In 2 Kings 24, we read about the fall of Jerusalem. We see that Jehoiakim and later his son Jehoiachin, the successors of Josiah, both turn away from faith in the Lord and do what is evil in his sight.

- As God promised, due to the sins of Manasseh, Jerusalem is delivered into the hand of the Babylonians. Nebuchadnezzar is going to bring into exile the servants of the king. First, he exiles the strongest of the people. He takes Jehoiachin "and all the princes, and all the mighty men of valor, ten thousand captives, and all the craftsmen and the smiths" (2 Kings 24:14). Only the poor and weak are left.

- Nebuchadnezzar makes Jehoiachin's uncle Mattaniah a puppet king, changing his name to Zedekiah.

- Soon, we will begin hearing from the prophets. We will go back to when Isaiah and Jeremiah are preaching, warning the people about the whole story we just heard about the bad kings and the people falling away from faith.

- The people continue to be unfaithful, though God continues to be faithful.

Take It to **Prayer**

Father in heaven, we thank you and give you praise. Thank you for your wisdom, your wisdom that goes forth from you, your wisdom which created the world. It is true, Lord God, that when we listen to you and we keep your ways, we are happy. We are blessed. Help us to hear instruction and be wise. Help us to watch daily at the gates of wisdom. Help us to find wisdom and therefore find life and obtain favor from you. Thank you, Lord. Thank you for this opportunity and thank you for this day. Once again, we pray this all in Jesus' name. Amen.

Dive **Deeper**

What were the conditions *of the exile?*

When the Babylonians destroyed Jerusalem in 587 BC, all but the poorest people were exiled to Babylon (see 2 Kings 25:11-12) for approximately seventy years. Then Cyrus the Great of Persia, Babylon's conqueror, let them return to Jerusalem.

During their exile in Babylon, Jeremiah assured the people that the Lord would be with them, and he encouraged them to serve the Babylonians until the Lord would restore them (see Jeremiah 24; 29:1-14). Many enjoyed relative freedom and wealth, and some, like Daniel, rose to prominent political positions within the royal court. Later, when the Persians took control, people such as Mordecai, Esther, and Nehemiah found themselves in key positions to help God's people, as Jeremiah advised. While they suffered physically and emotionally, they adapted themselves to their foreign exile.

It is thought that this is when synagogues were first established, so that the Jews in exile could observe the Sabbath and religious feasts, practice circumcision, and offer prayers as a substitute for worship in the Temple. One significant change for the Jews in exile was their forced exposure to a new language—Aramaic.

–Jeff Cavins

Reflect on the **Word**

- Over the course of salvation history, God's people were slaves in Egypt, but they were set free from their slavery by the hand of the Lord, who led them through the wilderness to the Promised Land with Moses and Joshua. In the Promised Land, the Lord gave them judges then anointed kings.

- We have seen the ways God continues to call his people to himself. Now, at the conclusion of 2 Kings and 2 Chronicles, we see the people are being exiled from their own land to Babylon.

- The ten tribes of the former Northern Kingdom are gone. The two tribes in the south, Judah and Benjamin, are now in exile.

- Now we have King Zedekiah. The Chaldeans capture him and bring him to the king of Babylon. They kill the sons of Zedekiah before him and then blind him. The last thing Zedekiah sees is the death of his children.

- The book of 2 Chronicles ends with a word of hope. In 2 Chronicles 36:21, we read that these things were "to fulfil the word of the LORD by the mouth of Jeremiah, until the land had enjoyed its sabbaths. All the days that it lay desolate it kept sabbath, to fulfil seventy years."

- Jeremiah notes that the land will someday recover (see Jeremiah 29:10). Though God allows the people to go into exile due to their infidelity, he is going to bring them back one day.

- Tomorrow, we will begin walking with the prophets. We will double back to hear what the Lord was saying through them to get the attention of his people and win back their hearts.

Take It to **Prayer**

Father in heaven, we give you praise, and as we come to a conclusion of this portion of the story, we know that, Lord, when all things seem dark, especially in our lives, we recognize that they are truly dark. They can be real darkness, there is real death, there is real suffering, there is real destruction, and yet we keep walking. Lord God, you have given us the ability to continue to move and act in this world, to continue to cry out to you, to call out to you with our broken hearts, to cry out to you with our broken lives. Even in the midst of darkness, you give us the power to walk. Help us, Lord God. Help us to walk with hope, knowing that darkness is not dark for you, the end is not the end for you. Even the grave is not the end for you, because we know that you have conquered sin. You have conquered suffering. You have conquered death, by your death and your resurrection. So Lord God, like you will bring resurrection to the people of Israel, although it will take so long, bring resurrection to our lives. Bring healing to our lives. Restore us to our home. Restore us to your heart. In Jesus' name we pray. Amen.

Dive **Deeper**

TOMB OF KING CYRUS

This tomb in Iran is thought to be the final resting place of the Persian king Cyrus. (See 2 Chronicles 36.)

Reflect on the **Word**

- Isaiah is one of the major prophets. Isaiah preaches primarily to Judah, the Southern Kingdom. He speaks of times "in the days of Uzziah, Jotham, Ahaz, and Hezekiah, kings of Judah" (Isaiah 1:1). Here, we see that his ministry spans the lives of at least four kings.

- The prophets correct the people, telling both Israel and Judah to reform their ways or the Lord will allow them to be destroyed by their enemies. The prophets proclaim a common message: God wants to bless the entire world through his Chosen People. But they need to be faithful to him.

- In the first two chapters of Isaiah, we see that God wants the people to offer their worship with their whole hearts rather than just as empty rituals.

- In Isaiah 1, the Lord proclaims that though their sins are like scarlet, they shall be as white as snow. There is consolation even in condemnation. God continues to call his people back to himself.

- Isaiah 2 speaks of the Lord's universal kingdom: "The mountain of the house of the LORD shall be established as the highest of the mountains, and shall be raised above the hills; and all the nations shall flow to it, and many peoples shall come, and say: 'Come, let us go up to the mountain of the LORD, to the house of the God of Jacob'" (Isaiah 2:2-3). This will be fulfilled in Jesus, through the Church he establishes.

- Tobit is from the kingdom of Israel. He is faithful and continues to worship even when Israel turns away from the Lord.

- Tobit chooses to perform corporal works of mercy, including caring for the poor and those who have died. He is a righteous man.

- Though he is faithful to the Lord, he is exiled. Nonetheless, Tobit 1 and 2 show us that, no matter who or what surrounds us, we can always do what God has asked us to do.

Take It to **Prayer**

Father in heaven, we give you praise. We thank you for this new step, this new day, this day 192. And we get to enter into two new books and not only two new books—the books of the prophets and also this book of Tobit. For many people who are listening, they have never heard your Word in this way before. And so we give you thanks for that. We give you thanks for the opportunity, like Tobit, to seek righteousness and to seek doing what is right, to try to be faithful no matter where we are living. Lord God, please help us to be faithful no matter where we are living, no matter who we are living with, no matter the people, the nation, the family, the roommate, whoever it is that we are living with, Lord God. Help us to remain faithful to you in all things, in all places, at all times. In Jesus' name we pray. Amen.

Dive **Deeper**

Did the events *recorded in Tobit actually happen?*

The events written about in the book of Tobit are not necessarily historical, although the book is set in an identifiable historical period—the time of the Assyrian exile. We do not know if there actually was a Tobit, a Tobias, or a Sarah, although there could have been. In other words, the story of Tobit may, indeed, be an account of actual events or simply a divinely inspired story to teach us theological truths.

As modern readers, we might think that a biblical book is true only if its contents are historically or scientifically accurate. But the intent of the author may not have been to write history at all. The stories in Tobit are meant to teach us, and we must try to discover the author's intention in order to see the truths he is trying to convey. We know that the book of Tobit is inerrant and divinely inspired because it is in the canon of Sacred Scripture.

–Kara Logan

Reflect on the **Word**

- Today, we will discuss why the book of Tobit is found only in Catholic Bibles. First, let's take a look at what are known as the "deuterocanonical" books of Scripture.

- There are seven deuterocanonical books: Tobit, Judith, Baruch, Ecclesiasticus (also known as Sirach), Wisdom, and 1 and 2 Maccabees. (Certain additions to the books of Esther and Daniel are also considered deuterocanonical.)

- Since Catholic Bibles include these seven books, they have a total of seventy-three books. Non-Catholic Bibles have sixty-six.

- When Jesus called his apostles, he gave them authority to teach and sanctify in his name (see Matthew 16:18-19). So the early Church determined the *canon* or definitive list of the inspired books of the Bible based on the authority given it by Christ.

- The deuterocanonical books are found in the Septuagint version of the Old Testament, which was translated from Hebrew into Greek in the third century BC.

- This was the Greek version of the Hebrew Scriptures that was used in the time of the apostles. When the New Testament authors quote the Old Testament, they are usually quoting from the Septuagint.

- At the Council of Rome in AD 382, the Church gave us the canon of the books of the Bible—the seventy-three books of the Old and New Testaments found in Catholic Bibles today.

- Until the Protestant Reformation in the sixteenth century, every Bible had all seventy-three books. Martin Luther and other Protestants, who did not accept the authority of the Catholic Church, removed the seven deuterocanonical books from their Bibles, choosing not to follow the Septuagint version. (Actually, some Protestant Bibles today include these seven books in a separate section called the "Apocrypha.")

Take It to **Prayer**

Father in heaven, we thank you and give you praise. We know that you invite us, you command us, you tell us to seek wisdom and to avoid foolishness. And so not only in the book of Proverbs do we have this sense of, like, OK, Lord, you remind us that, yes, so many voices are calling to us, so many voices are saying, "Hey! Over here! Over here! Over here! Come over here. Give us your attention. Give us your heart. Give us your mind. Give us your life." Because everything that takes our attention is taking our life. Everything that we give a minute of our attention to, we have given a minute of our lives to, a minute of our hearts to. And so, God, help us to be wise. Help us to not turn to every foolish voice, every foolish opportunity, but help us only listen to those wise voices in our lives. Help us only turn to the people that we know are wise, especially your Word, Lord God. We thank you for your Word because it is your Word that gives life. It is your Spirit that gives life. And so we give these minutes, we give this day, we give our heart to your Word, to your life, to your Spirit, and to your wisdom. Help us to always walk in your Spirit and always walk in your wisdom. In Jesus' name we pray. Amen.

Dive **Deeper**

So many voices and distractions threaten our focus, but the Lord's voice is the one we should pay attention to. Identify one thing in your life that you can change this week to cut down on distractions and keep your eyes on the Lord, and make that change!

Reflect on the **Word**

- In Isaiah 5, we see that God builds a vineyard—a metaphor for the people of Israel, whom he brings out of slavery in Egypt and makes fruitful. Yet, after planting choice grapes, God finds wild grapes instead. In Judah, the people of God do not bring forth the fruit for which he has set them apart.

- In the beginning of Isaiah 6, we read that Isaiah is commissioned as a prophet and beholds the glory of the Lord. He sees the seraphim, each of which has six wings. Symbolically, their feet and eyes are covered because they are in the presence of the Lord.

- They cry out, "Holy, holy, holy is the LORD of hosts; the whole earth is full of his glory" (Isaiah 6:3). As Catholics, we know these words from the Mass: the *Sanctus*—"Holy, Holy, Holy"—which we proclaim right before Jesus becomes present in the Holy Eucharist.

- When Isaiah experiences this vision, he laments, "Woe is me! For I am lost" (Isaiah 6:5). This is the experience of coming into the presence of the living God.

- This reminds us of when Jesus gets into Simon Peter's boat, and they have an overflowing catch of fish. Peter falls to his knees and says, "Depart from me, for I am a sinful man, O Lord" (Luke 5:8). Jesus then proclaims that he will make the apostles "fishers of men."

- Despite God's infinite holiness and our finite weakness, he calls us near. This is what Isaiah experiences in the Lord's presence.

- An angel takes a burning coal from the heavenly altar and touches Isaiah on the lips with it. The early Church Fathers saw this as a "type"—as a foreshadowing—of the Mass. After we proclaim, "Holy, holy, holy," we fall to our knees and then receive the "burning coal" of the Eucharist in our mouths. We experience a transformation by coming into contact with the Lord God himself.

- God then asks, "Whom shall I send?" Isaiah replies, "Here am I! Send me" (Isaiah 6:8). At the end of Mass, the celebrant says, "Go in peace, glorifying the Lord by your life." We have come into God's presence, fallen to our knees, and received the Lord himself in the Holy Eucharist; we have been transformed. Now, we are called to go and declare Jesus to the world.

Take It to **Prayer**

Father in heaven, we give you praise and thanks. We thank you so much. Thank you so much for your holiness. Thank you for your transcendence. Thank you for your omnipotence. Thank you for the fact that you are sovereign, Lord God. You are sovereign over all. And you are awe-inspiring. You are awesome and awful in the best possible way, Lord God. You inspire us, and we are full of awe in your presence and in the presence of your Word, Lord God, as you continue to speak to us these days. We ask that you please open our eyes that we may see and return to you. Open our ears that we may hear and return to you. Open our hearts that we can understand, our minds that we can understand and come back to you. In Jesus' name we pray. Amen.

Dive **Deeper**

Did Raphael tell a lie in Tobit 5:12?

In short, no. It is impossible for an angel to lie. Yet, in Tobit 5:12, Raphael says that he is one of Tobit's relatives. Only after his mission is complete does Raphael reveal his identity: "I will now declare the whole truth to you and I will not conceal anything" (Tobit 12:11). When Tobit and Tobias hear this, they fall to the ground. If Raphael had revealed his identity at first, perhaps Tobias would have been too terrified to go with him.

Raphael conceals his identity from Tobit by taking on the human form of one of Tobit's relatives to complete his mission. Similarly, one can say that he or she is a certain character in a play, for instance, and not be telling a lie. For, in a way, one is that character in that play. Similarly, Raphael can say he is "Azarias the son of the great Ananias."

St. Thomas Aquinas, discussing lying, says that when Jacob calls himself Esau, in this instance his words have a mystical sense. Perhaps we could say too that Raphael's words have a mystical sense and are meant to convey some truth about his mission and "signify a mystery."*

–Kara Logan

---

* Aquinas, *Summa Theologica*, II-II.110.3.3.

Reflect on the **Word**

- In Isaiah 7 and 8 we have a lesson of trust and expectation. Matthew tells us this is a foreshadowing of Jesus, Immanuel, God with us (see Matthew 1:22-23).

- Ahaz, son of Jotham, grandson of Uzziah, is now the king of Judah. He is not a good king. Rezin, the king of Syria, and Pekah, the king of Israel, have entered into an alliance, and they are coming to wage war against Judah (see 2 Kings 16:5).

- Isaiah tells Ahaz that the Lord wants to fight for him, defeat his enemies, and protect his people, so he should ask for a sign. Ahaz says he will not ask for a sign because he does not want to tempt the Lord. While Ahaz's reply sounds like humility, he says this because he knows he will make an alliance with the king of Assyria. With the Assyrians, he believes he does not need God.

- Isaiah responds to Ahaz's lack of trust with a prophecy: "Therefore the Lord himself will give you a sign. Behold, a virgin shall conceive and bear a son, and shall call his name Immanu-el" (Isaiah 7:14).

- In Tobit 7, we read that Raguel, the father of Sarah, lets Tobias know that his daughter has been married seven times, and each night her husband has been killed by the demon Asmodeus before the couple could consummate their relationship.

- The Lord has already sent Raphael to chase away the demon. Here, we see the power of the Lord and his angels over demons. Jesus gives authority to cast out demons to his apostles.

- In Tobit 8, we read that Tobias and Sarah are married and go into their wedding chamber. As in the Song of Solomon, Tobias loves and desires Sarah, but he first sees her as his sister.

- Tobias and Sarah are a beautiful example of spouses who pray together. They praise God for his goodness, and they pray that they treat each other well and grow old together in love.

Take It to **Prayer**

Lord God, we give you praise and thank you so much. Thank you for your wisdom and thank you for continuing to reveal your heart to us. Thank you for calling us to be images of your love in this world. We ask that you please help us to trust in you above all things in everything. Lord God, we ask you, help us to trust you in absolutely everything. In Jesus' name we pray. Amen.

Dive **Deeper**

Tobias and Sarah show us the importance of prayer in marriage. If you are married, pray with your spouse today. The prayer of Tobias is a great place to start. If you are not married, pray for married couples that God may strengthen their bond and that his love may grow strong in their union.

Reflect on the **Word**

- We need to consider the context of Isaiah 9. Israel will be destroyed when the Assyrians come into the north, to the land of Zebulun and the land of Naphtali. Later, the Lord will make glorious the land beyond the Jordan.

- After Jesus is baptized by John and is tempted by Satan for forty days in the wilderness, he goes up to the land of Zebulun and the land of Naphtali. Here, he fulfills what Isaiah prophesied. (See Matthew 4:12-16.)

- After Jesus goes here, he calls Simon, Andrew, James, and John to follow him. Ultimately, he will call twelve apostles, a number which symbolizes the reconstituted twelve tribes of Israel, under Jesus as King. This fulfillment begins in the land of Galilee of the Gentiles. People who walked in darkness have seen a great light.

- Isaiah 9:6 says, "For to us a child is born, to us a son is given; and the government will be upon his shoulder, and his name will be called 'Wonderful Counselor, Mighty God, Everlasting Father, Prince of Peace.' Of the increase of his government and of peace there will be no end."

- In Isaiah 10:5, God says he will use Assyria as a tool—"the rod of my anger"— to bring about justice.

- At the end of Isaiah 10, we see that there will be a remnant in Israel. Some of the Lord's people will be left there to accomplish his will and bring about a worldwide blessing.

- Raphael explains to Tobias and Tobit that prayer must be accompanied by fasting (self-denial), almsgiving (taking care of those around us), and righteousness (doing what God has commanded us to do).

Take It to **Prayer**

Father in heaven, we give you praise and glory, and we thank you so much. We thank you for your word, and we thank you for your wisdom that you give to us through these wise sayings of Solomon in the book of Proverbs. Because we know it is true that you call us to not mess around with evil. You call us to choose the good with our whole heart, to choose you with our whole heart, mind, soul, and strength, to love you with everything we have and everything we are— because hatred stirs up strife, but love covers all offenses. Help us to love you well. Help us to love you wisely in this world that can often be so confusing and so tricky, to know how to love the people around us well, to know how to love you well, and to let people into our lives, to let them know us, to let them love us. So we ask for your help, Lord. Help us to love well. Help us to be loved well. And help us to be an image of you in this world every day of our lives. In Jesus' name we pray. Amen.

Dive **Deeper**

CHANT FOR
CHRISTMAS DAY

This medieval manuscript (circa AD 1500) shows the beginning of a prayer from the liturgy of Christmas Day, which sees Isaiah 9:6 ("For to us a child is born ...") as fulfilled in Jesus.

Reflect on the **Word**

- Recall that Isaiah is present when King Hezekiah turns to the Lord to be saved from the Assyrians. The king goes to the Temple and asks God for deliverance—and God saves Judah. (See 2 Kings 19.) But exile is yet to come.

- Isaiah calls the people to repentance and warns them of what will happen if they refuse. He also offers words of consolation, telling them that though the Lord will punish them for their sins, he has not abandoned them. They will return.

- Isaiah 11:1 says, "There shall come forth a shoot from the stump of Jesse, and a branch shall grow out of his roots." Jesse is the father of David, and God has promised that the kingdom of David will endure forever and that the Messiah will be one of his descendants.

- Only a stump will be left of the destroyed kingdom—but a shoot will come forth from it. All is not lost.

- "And the Spirit of the LORD shall rest upon him, the spirit of wisdom and understanding, the spirit of counsel and might, the spirit of knowledge and the fear of the LORD" (Isaiah 11:2). This is a prophecy of Jesus. Remember, when Jesus goes into the synagogue in Nazareth, he unrolls the scroll and proclaims from Isaiah 61, "The Spirit of the Lord is upon me ..." (See Luke 4:16-19; Isaiah 61:1-2.)

- This is the "good news." We have been reading the story of God's promises and his people's faithlessness. Jesus comes and says that what Isaiah proclaimed seven hundred years before has arrived.

- In Tobit 13, we see Tobit's prayer of rejoicing. Tobit shows that even in exile, he can praise God—and even more so when in exile, so that those around him will come to know who God is.

Take It to **Prayer**

Father in heaven, we give you praise and glory. We thank you so much for this opportunity once again, so many days in a row, to be able to ... whether or not in a row, Lord God, you have given us this opportunity to come back and allow you to speak to us. To speak to us and to give us your wisdom, to speak to us and to call us back to you, to speak to us and to remind us of the great consolation you have in store for us in our lives. And so we give you praise, and we just offer you our thanks. We offer you praise because like we heard yesterday, "Keep the secrets of a king but give God exultant praise, exultant glory." And, God, may you be exalted in praise and glory. In Jesus' name we pray. Amen.

Dive **Deeper**

Return to Tobit's prayer of rejoicing in exile in Tobit 13. Pray it from your heart. Praise God in the midst of both the joys and sufferings of your life.

Reflect on the **Word**

- In Isaiah 14:4, the prophet speaks about the king of Babylon, exclaiming how the mighty has fallen. He then says, "How you are fallen from heaven, O Day Star, son of Dawn! How you are cut down to the ground, you who laid the nations low! You said in your heart, 'I will ascend to heaven; above the stars of God'" (Isaiah 14:12-13). This is both a direct prophecy against the king of Babylon and a prophecy with a deeper, spiritual meaning.

- Remember—the prophets do not simply foretell the future. They speak the truths of the Lord on his behalf. Many prophecies have both a historical meaning and a spiritual meaning.

- The translation of "O Day Star" is "Lucifer"—the name for Satan. Lucifer, once an angel of light, freely chose to rebel against the Lord in his pride. Both the king of Babylon and Lucifer proclaim that they will not serve but seek to make themselves like God. In Isaiah 14, then, the prophecy is about both the king of Babylon, who will soon be toppled, and Lucifer, who will ultimately be toppled.

- The prophet Joel preaches to Judah. Joel 2:11 says, "The Lord utters his voice before his army, for his host is exceedingly great ... For the day of the Lord is great and very awesome; who can endure it?" The Lord allows these things to call the people of Judah to repentance. Whenever God allows tragedy to befall his people, he is always seeking to get their attention. The "day of the Lord" brings justice and righteousness—for vindication, but always to bring his people back to him.

- The Lord says, "Return to me with all your heart, with fasting, with weeping, and with mourning; and tear your hearts and not your garments" (Joel 2:12-13). He is calling the people not just to tear their garments and *look* holy, but to tear their hearts and *be* holy. In other words, do not just look like a good worshipper, actually worship; do not just look like someone who repents, actually repent.

- Joel 2:25 tells us, "I will restore to you the years which the swarming locust has eaten." The promise of God, when we come back to him and are his again, is not just a restoration of our possessions, but of our time—all that we lost and more.

- He has this same promise and invitation for us today. We are not called to be people who look like we love God, but to be people who actually do love God.

Take It to **Prayer**

Father in heaven, we give you praise, and with our mouths we want to give you glory, and we want to say words that honor you, God, because you are so good. You love us so well, and you love us so fully every single day. So please, Lord, help us to know your love. Help us to know your name. And help us to know your voice. And help us always to speak of your love, to speak of your name, and to speak with the voice that you would speak, because it is true that we need to guard our words, and we need to guide our words. Another way to say it, Father, I just ask that you guard my words and that you guide my words. In Jesus' name we pray. Amen.

Dive **Deeper**

We are called to be people who actually love God, not people who merely look like we love God. Pray with Joel 2:12-13 today and ask for God's grace to worship him in spirit and truth.

Reflect on the **Word**

- An important prophecy from yesterday in Joel 2 explains what will happen "in those days": God will pour out his Spirit on all flesh, and their sons and daughters shall prophesy. Old men shall dream dreams, and young men shall see visions. This will come to pass on the feast of Pentecost. When Peter calls the people to repentance, he even quotes from the book of Joel. (See Acts 2:16-21.)

- Joel speaks about what will happen after the day of the Lord, when justice will once again reign. His words seem to be contrary to Isaiah 2, where we read that the people will beat swords into plowshares and pruning hooks—but Joel says to prepare for war.

- Ultimately, we are meant to live in peace—with God, one another, and ourselves. But Ecclesiastes tells us that there is a time for war (see Ecclesiastes 3:8). As long as we live in a violent world, there are times when we have to be warriors in this spiritual battle. This is the cost of living in a broken, sinful world.

- Our call is not necessarily to take up arms against others in physical violence. Remember that St. Paul says our battle is not with flesh and blood but with principalities and powers, with the demons and dark forces that fight against us (see Ephesians 6:12).

- The justice of God is always oriented toward conversion. As Isaiah 17:7 says, the pagan people living in Syria in the region of Damascus will regard their Maker. They will remember that there is a God in heaven, and their eyes will look to the Holy One of Israel.

- This is all to get their attention. As C. S. Lewis says, while we can pay no attention to pleasure, "pain insists upon being attended to. God whispers to us in our pleasures ... but shouts in our pain." Pain is God's "megaphone to rouse a deaf world."*

- Suffering can be prayer for all of us: "Lord, I do not want pain, but if that is needed for me to listen to you, help me to hear you. When a storm comes, Lord, help me to see your face in the midst of it."

---

* C. S. Lewis, *The Problem of Pain* (New York: HarperSanFrancisco, 1996), 91.

Take It to **Prayer**

Father in heaven, we give you praise and glory. We thank you so much, God, for your Word. We thank you for the prophet Joel, who was with us for only two days. And yet, your prophet Joel not only prophesied that yes, young men would see visions and dream dreams—that's fulfilled in the New Covenant— but also he calls us to repentance just like your prophet Isaiah called the people of Judah and us to repentance as well. Help us to give our hearts to you more fully this day and every day. In Jesus' name we pray. Amen.

Dive **Deeper**

What does it mean to you that pain is God's "megaphone to rouse a deaf world"? If you are experiencing pain in your life right now, how do you think God might be speaking to you in the midst of it?

Reflect on the **Word**

- The oracles in Isaiah 18 and 19 are a call to get rid of idols. The Lord says he will stir up Egyptian against Egyptian, city against city, kingdom against kingdom. The false gods of the Egyptians must be defeated. Once again, God calls his people back to himself.

- At the end of Isaiah 19, God says he will accomplish good through Israel's alliance with Egypt and Assyria, even though this seems impossible. Egypt and Assyria have done so much evil, but it shows that we have a God who restores us.

- In Romans 5, St. Paul says that, even while we are still sinners, God proves his love for us in the death of Jesus. The Lord died for his enemies to make them his friends—his sons and daughters.

- In Isaiah 20, Isaiah lives out the words of prophecy. The Lord comes to the prophet and tells him to loosen the sackcloth from his loins and take the shoes from his feet. For the next three years, he walks naked and barefoot as a sign against Egypt and Ethiopia. Soon, the king of Assyria will destroy Ethiopia and Egypt.

- In the book of Nahum, Nahum shows that the Lord is grieved by the suffering and death of the innocent.

- God will judge those who use violence to dominate others. But his judgment is always oriented toward justice.

- We pray for justice in our lives and in our world.

Take It to **Prayer**

Father in heaven, we give you praise and glory always. Every single day, Lord, we get to once again lift up your name. We get to declare your mighty deeds. We get to declare what you have done for us. So Lord, let this be a day like all those other days where we get to declare your works and praise you and praise your name. Let's speak of your name to those around us and speak of your name to those who know you and those who do not yet know you. Because you are a God of redemption. You are a God of mercy. You are a God who can enter into this broken world, and you can bring healing. Lord God, we ask that you please bring us healing. Bring our hearts healing this day and every day. In Jesus' name we pray. Amen.

Dive **Deeper**

Jesus, who is God, died for you, to make you a son or daughter of God. Spend some time in prayer today gazing upon a crucifix or image of the Passion and death of Jesus. Meditate on the depth of his love for you.

Reflect on the **Word**

- Isaiah says, "Go, set a watchman, let him announce what he sees" (Isaiah 21:6). This is the role of the prophet—to be a watchman, pointing out dangers. Many have suffered and been destroyed because there was no one on the watchtower to warn them about what was coming.

- In Isaiah 22, we see two individuals, Shebna and Eliakim. Shebna is the one who is over the household. Shebna's role, designated by the Hebrew term *al habayit*, is basically to be the prime minister of the kingdom. So when the king is away, Shebna has all of the authority of the king.

- Shebna uses his power to exalt himself, and he makes himself his own tomb in a rock. The Lord says he has misused his authority and power, so he will thrust him out of his station and bring in Eliakim, the son of Hilkiah.

- In Matthew 16:13, Jesus asks his disciples, "Who do men say that the Son of Man is?" Simon proclaims that he is the Messiah, the holy one of God. In reply, Jesus says that Simon's name is now *Peter* ("rock") and that he will build his Church upon this rock. Jesus says to Peter, "I will give you the keys of the kingdom of heaven, and whatever you bind on earth shall be bound in heaven, and whatever you loose on earth shall be loosed in heaven" (Matthew 16:19).

- Here we see the significance of Isaiah's words: "And I will place on his shoulder the key of the house of David; he shall open and none shall shut; and he shall shut, and none shall open" (Isaiah 22:22).

- Matthew makes it clear that Jesus is the King who will restore the kingdom that has been scattered. In his kingdom, just as in Judah's kingdom, there is the role of *al habayit*. Jesus, the King, has made Peter the first *al habayit* of his kingdom.

- As bishop of Rome, Peter and his successors are each the *al habayit* of the Church, the father of the house. Isaiah 22:21 says, "He shall be a father to the inhabitants of Jerusalem and to the house of Judah." The *al habayit* serves not only by governing, but by guiding, as a spiritual father.

- Isaiah 22 is fulfilled in Matthew 16. Catholics, then, did not invent the papacy in the days of the early Church or in the Middle Ages. The role of the pope comes directly from the Old Testament.

Take It to **Prayer**

Father in heaven, we give you praise and glory. We thank you so much for your faithfulness. We thank you for your goodness, your justice, and your righteousness. Help us to live in righteousness. Help us to live in right relationship with each other, and with you above all things. Lord God, help us to have right hearts in ourselves and not be our own enemies, our own worst enemies. But Lord God, help us to have that knowledge, that wisdom that we actually do speak what is true, we live what we know to be true, and we cling to you above everything else in this world. We make this prayer in the name of Jesus Christ, our Lord. Amen.

Dive **Deeper**

What is the al habayit?

In the kingdom of David, there was a position known as the *al habayit*. This man was appointed by the king to be prime minister with authority over the royal house. This role was essential to the continuity of the kingdom if the king was seriously ill or killed in battle.

In Isaiah 22:15-25, we see a description of the role of the *al habayit*. He was entrusted with the key to the house of the king; what he allowed was allowed, and what he forbade was forbidden. In Isaiah 22, we read how Shebna, who held this position at that time, was removed due to his pride.

In the New Testament, the keys of the kingdom were given by Jesus to the apostle Peter in Matthew 16. Peter would lead the Church after Jesus ascended into heaven. Over the centuries, Peter's successors, the bishops of Rome (the popes), have held these keys of authority over the Church of Christ.

–Jeff Cavins

Reflect on the **Word**

- Isaiah prophesies that Tyre, one of the coastal towns on the Mediterranean Sea, will be destroyed. But in Isaiah 23:18, we are told that Tyre's "merchandise and her hire" will ultimately "be dedicated to the LORD." This is a prophecy about the restoration of Tyre after seventy years, but it also points to a New Testament reality.

- As noted in Acts 21:4, St. Paul found many Christians in Tyre. Ultimately, Tyre found a purpose in belonging to the Lord.

- Isaiah 24 speaks about God's impending judgment. "Terror, and the pit, and the snare" will come upon the people (see Isaiah 24:17). This judgment will touch even kings.

- This is both a word of warning and a word of promise. Though it is a condemnation for those who fall away from the Lord and rebel against him, it is also a promise that God will again reign in Jerusalem and in Judah.

- Habakkuk points out that there are people who have turned away from the Lord and who abuse each other. He speaks of the wickedness of this world and says that the Lord will soon address it.

- In Habakkuk 2, we have God's reply to Habakkuk: woes to those who practice unjust economics, employ slave labor, use other people, make neighbors drink, and trust in idols.

- Habakkuk makes clear that what will happen in Babylon will happen to every nation that rebels against the Lord. Here, there is a lesson for us.

- The Lord not only brings judgment but brings about his own glory, so that he can be known.

Take It to **Prayer**

Father in heaven, we give you praise and glory, and we thank you. Thank you for your wisdom. Again, every time we hear your Word, Lord, in Proverbs, your Word coming from Solomon ... who was a wise man in his mind and not necessarily always wise in his actions, but who continually reminds us that those who choose you, even if they are devoid of everything else, are choosing the right path. Even those who have wealth, even those who have power in this life— ultimately we fall into your hands. And so we ask not just for more wealth or not just for more power, but we ask for right relationship with you, right relationship with each other. And even in our hearts, Lord God, we ask for right relationship in ourselves, that we can be the kind of men and women who not only say yes to you with our minds, and say yes to you with our voices, but say yes to you with our entire lives. Help us to say yes to you, to your wisdom, and to walk in wisdom this day and every day. In Jesus' name we pray. Amen.

Dive **Deeper**

Hearing the woes surrounding God's judgment gives each of us a good opportunity to examine our own consciences. There are many good, Catholic examinations of conscience available online to help us sincerely look at the areas in our lives where we need God's mercy and to turn back to the Lord with repentance.

Reflect on the **Word**

- In Isaiah 25, 26, and 27, we see praise for delivery from oppression. This is expressed right in the middle of the call to repentance and promise of judgment. Isaiah says clearly that the people will be brought into captivity in the land of Babylon. Yet Isaiah 25 says that God will swallow up death and wipe away tears from all faces. This is the promise of the day of the Messiah, of redemption.

- God has created us and redeemed us. In our brokenness, God has met us with his mercy.

- Isaiah 25:9 is the promise of God seven hundred years before Jesus' birth. "Behold, this is our God" is what we say about Jesus. John the Baptist at the river Jordan says, "Behold, the Lamb of God, who takes away the sin of the world!" (John 1:29). At every Mass, we say, "Behold the Lamb of God, behold him who takes away the sins of the world." This is our God, who has come to save us, so let us rejoice and be glad for this gift.

- Habakkuk is preaching about the reality of Babylon's destruction of the kingdom of Judah. But we hear Habakkuk's prayer and God's answer, which is about redemption. For God wants to bring his people back.

- It will be a new exodus as those enslaved and exiled will be brought back from slavery. It is God's promise of faithfulness.

- In the meantime, we are to steadfastly wait, knowing and trusting that God will bring us home from exile. We are to do this "though the fig tree does not blossom, nor fruit be on the vines" (Habakkuk 3:17).

- Habakkuk 3:18 tells us, "Yet I will rejoice in the Lord, I will joy in the God of my salvation." Even though nothing is going right, God has promised. Even though the good that was promised has not arrived, we are still called to rejoice in the Lord. He is our strength and our salvation.

Take It to **Prayer**

Father in heaven, we give you praise, and we thank you. We thank you because, Lord, in all of this we want to be counted among those who are righteous, not those who are wicked, not those who are unfaithful. And yet, we strive to be wise. We strive to be good. We strive to belong to you. But so often, Lord, we fail to belong to you. We fail to be good. We fail to be yours. And so we ask you that when we are wicked, when we are treacherous, when we are not righteous, we ask you to make us so. Because only you, only you and your grace can make us the people that we are called to be, the people that you redeemed us to be. Lord God, what Jesus accomplished your Holy Spirit makes present, and so we trust in your Spirit to come to us now and to make us new. In Jesus' name we pray. Amen.

Destruction of Leviathan, Gustave Doré

Dive **Deeper**

LEVIATHAN

This image shows God pointing a heavenly sword at Leviathan, a monstrous sea serpent often associated with chaos and opposition to God. In texts like Isaiah 27, God's defeat of the serpent signifies Israel's redemption.

Reflect on the **Word**

- In Isaiah 28, we see a reference to drunkenness. The Bible says that the blessing of wine gives joy to men's hearts (see Psalm 104:15), but drunkenness is sinful (see 1 Corinthians 6:10).

- Created in God's image and likeness, we have an intellect and a will. Original sin, though, darkened our intellect, weakened our will, and led to *concupiscence*, an attraction to sin. Drunkenness emphasizes all three of these consequences of the Fall.

- The Lord says, "Behold, I am laying in Zion for a foundation a stone, a tested stone, a precious cornerstone, of a sure foundation" (Isaiah 28:16). In the New Testament, 1 Peter 2:6 speaks about Jesus as this precious cornerstone and foundation.

- The prophet Zephaniah prophesies in the days of Josiah, the young king who restores worship in the kingdom of Judah (see 2 Kings 22–23).

- In chapter 1, Zephaniah accuses the people of Judah of many evils. They have fallen into idolatry; they have failed to pray; their leaders are bad; they are superstitious; and they believe that no judgment will come upon them for their actions. All of these indictments touch on the heart of their relationship with the Lord.

- Zephaniah proclaims that the Day of the Lord is coming, so the people should seek the Lord and his righteousness with humility.

- We, too, are in the spiritual battle between God and the principalities of this earth. As we await the Day of the Lord, we are called to seek justice. That is the message of Zephaniah and all the prophets—for their time and for today.

Take It to **Prayer**

Father in heaven, we give you praise, and we thank you for your Word. We thank you for continuing to speak to us and continuing to call us to be yours. We know that you are present in all things and that your judgment on the world and your judgment on our lives, our actions is good, is true, is fair, is just. Because you are good, and you are true, and you are fair, and you are just. Lord, you know the secrets of our hearts. You know our weaknesses. You know our strengths. You know the wounds that we carry, that no one else knows. And because of that, you can judge us rightly, and you love us. Therefore, you want the best for us. God, I ask that you please use this day. Use what happens in our lives today, whether they be positive things or negative things, whether they be joyous things or sufferings. Use the moments of this day, the interactions of this day, to call us back to you. Let the joys remind us of your goodness. Let our sufferings remind us of our need for you. Let every moment be a reminder of how much you love us and how much we are yours, how deeply we belong to you. In Jesus' name we pray. Amen.

Dive **Deeper**

Did the prophet *Isaiah write the entire book attributed to him?*

There is some debate about the authorship of the book of Isaiah among modern biblical scholars. Many of these scholars divide the book into three parts and suggest each part was written at a different time by a different author.

However, as noted by scholars John Bergsma and Brant Pitre in *A Catholic Introduction to the Bible: The Old Testament,* various books of the Old and New Testaments attribute the authorship of the entire book of Isaiah to the prophet Isaiah himself. Bergsma and Pitre also note that the historian Josephus wrote in his *Antiquities* that the reason that Cyrus allowed the Jews to return to the land was because he read the section in Isaiah that prophesied concerning him. We thus have evidence from a first-century Jewish source that Isaiah was written before the time of Cyrus.

In the end, such questions are of interest to scholars but should not concern us. Regardless of the authorship of Isaiah—or any other book of Scripture, for that matter—it is divinely inspired.

–Kara Logan

Reflect on the **Word**

- In Isaiah 30, the prophet speaks of a rebellious people who carry out their own plan rather than God's will. Isaiah counsels Judah against making an alliance with foreign nations because the Lord wants to fight for his people.

- The Lord fought against the Egyptians to set the Israelites free from slavery— and he will fight for them again if they trust him.

- As chapter 30 continues, we read that the people will have adversity and affliction, but their eyes will be opened.

- Yesterday, in Zephaniah, we read about the condemnations of the people of Judah.

- As we see in Zephaniah 3:5, "the unjust knows no shame." Today, we live in a shameless culture, one that has largely abandoned the ways of the Lord.

- We should feel ashamed of our sins but not crippled by shame. For God has taken away the judgment against us. Isaiah prophesies of the coming of the Messiah. Jesus is the One who conquers sin through the Cross. When we acknowledge our shame, Jesus rejoices and turns our shame into praise and glory.

Take It to **Prayer**

Father in heaven, we give you praise and thank you. Thank you for this opportunity to be together. Thank you for your Word that you continue to speak to us. And thank you for the Holy Spirit that helps us to unpack and unlock your Word because of your teaching, your truth, and the way in which you reveal your heart through the Word that you have spoken to us through the prophets. Those here today, Isaiah and Zephaniah. And through even the wisdom of Solomon who assembled these pieces of wisdom so that we can understand and we can live our lives in a way that he failed to live his life. And we can be guided by your wisdom, by your truth, and by your Word. Thank you, Father. Help us to not only hear your Word, but to listen to it. Help us not only to know of it, but to accomplish it in our lives by your grace. In Jesus' name we pray. Amen.

Dive **Deeper**

Today, take Zephaniah's condemnations of the people of Judah to prayer. Consider them in light of your relationship with God. Do any call you to make changes in your life? If so, ask for the Lord's mercy and take a step in the right direction.

Reflect on the **Word**

- In Isaiah 32, we have the prophecy of a righteous king. This could be Hezekiah, who prayed before the Lord in the Temple as the Assyrians were threatening Jerusalem (see 2 Kings 19). Isaiah's prophecy could also apply to Josiah, the great-grandson of Hezekiah.

- Isaiah calls the people back to the Lord, telling them to wake up from their complacency and self-indulgence.

- Isaiah talks about the righteous judgment of the Lord against the nations that none will escape. Everyone and everything belongs to God—even those who do not believe in him.

- Baruch was a contemporary of Jeremiah. He might have even been Jeremiah's scribe. Baruch writes among the people exiled in Babylon.

- In Baruch, we read a letter to Jerusalem asking for prayers on behalf of Nebuchadnezzar, king of Babylon, and his son Belshazzar. In Romans 13, St. Paul speaks about respect for rulers. We should pray for rulers, even unjust ones (see 1 Timothy 2:1-2).

- In Baruch, the people confess their sins and admit that, though they knew the Law, they disobeyed the Lord. They lacked hearts willing to be changed to be what God called them to be. They pray for deliverance.

- The final line of Baruch 2 offers hope: "I will make an everlasting covenant with them to be their God and they shall be my people; and I will never again remove my people Israel from the land which I have given them."

Take It to **Prayer**

Father in heaven, we give you praise and glory. We ask you to please help us, once again. As we pray these Proverbs, we ask you to help us to become the people who are kind and the person who is righteous and the person who lives in right relationship with you. Help us to actually live in right relationship with you this day and every day. Lord God, help us to hear your words clearly. To understand them and understand not only how you spoke to your people Israel but also how you are speaking in your Scripture today, to us, to your people now. We bear your name like they bore your name. So please, as you were faithful with them, be faithful with us. And we give you praise, and we love you. We make this prayer in the mighty name of your Son, Jesus Christ, our Lord. Amen.

Dive **Deeper**

Why does God *tell his people to submit to the king of Babylon in Baruch 1?*

First, the king of Babylon is the temporal ruler of the Israelite people, and even if rulers are unjust, we are called to pray for them. But Baruch also tells the people to submit because this is the punishment for their disobedience. As we recall from Deuteronomy 31, the consequence of not obeying the Law is exile.

When children willingly accept the consequences of their actions, this is pleasing to their parents. Similarly, Baruch tells the people to humble themselves and undergo what the Lord has justly inflicted. It is pleasing to God if his people humbly acknowledge their sins and willingly endure the hardships that they rightly deserve. In doing so, they will gain again the favor of the Lord. In addition, Israel may win the favor of the king of Babylon and be a "light to the nations."

There is also a note of hope in Baruch. While God allows his people to be taken into exile, he offers a promise to one day bring them back into their land.

–Kara Logan

Reflect on the **Word**

- Isaiah 34 speaks about the Lord's wrath against the nations.

- Isaiah 35 describes how the Lord will come to save the people of Israel and how they shall see his glory. The prophets continually speak of the return of the Lord, who will bring salvation.

- When we hear of the Lord's coming, are we filled with excitement and hope or fear and dread? Our response is determined by our view of God and whether we have been living as the Lord asks us to live.

- Beginning in chapter 36, Isaiah retells the story we have already seen in Chronicles and Kings—Sennacherib's coming.

- In Baruch 3, the prophet writes about wisdom. The people perished through their folly.

- Baruch does not ignore the fact that Israel forgot the Lord. In doing so, they grieved him, and he handed them over to their enemies. But the Lord remembers them and comes to save them.

- Baruch exhorts the people—and us—to "take courage," to cry to God, and he will deliver them from the power of the enemy (Baruch 4:21).

Take It to **Prayer**

Father in heaven, we give you praise and glory. Lord, we love you today and every day. But, God, thank you so much for your Word. Thank you for your encouragement that you give to us from Baruch. Thank you even for the connections, I think, Lord God, that we get to make today in the book of the prophet Isaiah. And thank you for your willingness, for continuing to speak to us every single day. Even days when we miss days and when we have to pick it back up. Thank you for your faithfulness, because even on days when we don't listen, even on days when we choose to ignore your voice, you continue to speak, and you continue to bring us back to you. Lord God, help us on our worst day. Right now, O God, we pray for the worst day of our life, that even on that day we can hear your voice and on that day we can be faithful to your completely unstoppable and faithful love. In Jesus' name we pray. Amen.

Dive **Deeper**

What is your image of God? Have you been living as the Father is asking? Dwell on these questions in your prayer today. Ask for the grace to look for his return with hope.

Reflect on the **Word**

- We hear again in Isaiah the story of the king of Assyria, Sennacherib, who boasts that he will defeat Jerusalem as he has defeated the other nations. Hezekiah turns to the Lord, who hears his prayer for protection, deliverance, and a longer life.

- In Baruch 5, the prophet offers encouragement, as the Lord tells Jerusalem to take off the garment of sorrow and affliction and put on the robe of righteousness. God will redeem the people and bring them home; the time of exile will come to an end.

- Baruch 6 is a letter of Jeremiah to the captives. Through Baruch, Jeremiah reminds the people in Babylon that they will be tempted to worship the idols that surround them. He warns them not to turn away from the worship of the Lord, the one true God.

- We, too, can be tempted to turn away from the worship God has asked from us and to worship "false gods," to give power to superstitions. We should not be afraid of something that only has the power over us we give it.

- The prophet Baruch reminds the people in exile that they have a God who knows them—he is the true and living God, and they belong to him. So there is no reason to fear.

Take It to **Prayer**

Father in heaven, we give you praise and glory. We thank you for your Word. We thank you for revealing your heart to us, and we give you praise this day and every day, confident that you hear our prayers and you know our needs and you meet us now. In Jesus' name we pray. Amen.

Dive **Deeper**

TEMPLE OF BEL

This first-century temple, located in Palmyra, Syria, was dedicated to Bel, or Baal. Baruch 6 mentions Bel in its condemnation of idolatry.

Reflect on the **Word**

- Much of Isaiah 40 is proclaimed during the season of Advent: "A voice cries: 'In the wilderness prepare the way of the LORD'" (Isaiah 40:3).

- In these words, we recognize St. John the Baptist, who proclaims Jesus as the Lamb of God who takes away the sins of the world. He prepares people for the coming of Christ.

- Today, we are introduced to Ezekiel, who is not only a prophet but also a priest from the tribe of Levi. He too is taken into exile in Babylon.

- In the vision of the four figures, we have a description of someone seated on a throne. The exiles are away from Jerusalem and the Temple, away from the presence of the Lord. How could the Lord abide in Babylon? Yet God reveals to Ezekiel that he has gone with his people into exile; he has not abandoned them.

- The four living creatures have the faces of a man, a lion, an ox, and an eagle. The Church has interpreted that these faces allude to the Gospel writers.

- The man represents Matthew, for Matthew traces Jesus' genealogy back to Abraham, showing the unfolding of God's plan to send the Messiah, who became man and dwelt among us.

- The lion represents Mark, who shows that Jesus is the lion of Judah.

- The ox represents Luke, who speaks of sacrificial rites. Jesus' sacrifice on the Cross was priestly.

- The eagle represents John. He is like an eagle soaring. In the beginning of his Gospel he writes, "In the beginning was the Word, and the Word was with God, and the Word was God" (John 1:1).

Take It to **Prayer**

Father in heaven, we give you praise, and we thank you so much for your Word. Thank you for speaking to us. Thank you for coming to us and being among us. Thank you not only for being with us in our good days—in our days of strength, in our days of victory, in our days where we know that we belong, that we are loved—but also, Lord God, we thank you for being with us on those days where it is difficult to know if anyone notices. It is difficult to know if anyone knows us. It is difficult to know if anyone truly loves. You are the God who is so faithful that you love us when no one else does. You see us when no one else sees. You are with us when we are alone and no one else is with us. And so we thank you, and we give you praise because you do this. You love us solely out of the goodness of you: Father, Son, and Holy Spirit. And so we are so grateful, so thankful. We love you, God. Thank you for loving us. Receive our prayer and help us to love you better. In Jesus' name. Amen.

Dive **Deeper**

***What is the meaning** of the vision in Ezekiel 1?*

To understand the vision, it is important to understand that Ezekiel's message was intended for those in captivity in Babylon.

In his vision, Ezekiel describes seeing a heavenly chariot where God is enthroned. With the lofty chariot, Ezekiel sees shining wheels with eyes around the edges, and next to the wheels are four creatures with different faces—man, lion, eagle, and ox.

Some hold that the man, lion, eagle, and ox are suggestive of the Babylonian zodiac. The message to those in exile is that the Babylonian deities have not overcome the Lord, but God abides on high above the entire universe. Others believe that the four creatures are a foreshadowing of the writers of the four Gospels. Either way, the vision reminds the people that during times of turmoil and upheaval, God is always in control and is with them. He will restore them according to his promise.

–Jeff Cavins

Reflect on the **Word**

- As we read Isaiah and Ezekiel, we need to be aware of their different contexts. Isaiah writes before the Babylonian Exile, in the land of Judah. Ezekiel is writing during the Exile, in Babylon.

- The Babylonians exile the people of Israel in three waves. Ezekiel is taken in the second wave.

- When Isaiah is prophesying, the destruction of Jerusalem and the Exile have not yet happened. (The people have just been saved from the Assyrians.) Though Isaiah prophesies it will happen, he says that the Lord will restore his people and bring them back.

- Isaiah 42 is a prophecy of the Messiah, who will come for righteousness and mercy.

- Soon, we will hear about some strange things Ezekiel is commanded to do by the Lord in the sight of the people.

- God makes it clear that we are to speak the words he gives us to speak— and that we have no control over whether people heed them or not. We can only control what we ourselves do.

Take It to **Prayer**

Father in heaven, we give you praise, and we thank you. And we know that you are our Father. And so because you are our Father, you want us to be like your Son. You want us to be icons of Jesus Christ in this world, and we are not, because we go astray. We are not, because we don't trust you. We are not, because we don't love like you love. We don't love like Christ loves. And so we ask you to send your Spirit into our hearts—because we can't. We don't have the ability. We don't have the capacity to love as you love, to be as you are, and to live as Christ, your Son, lived, on our own. But with your help, we can do all things. If we remain in your Son, Jesus, we can accomplish your will by the power of your Holy Spirit. So please, once again, Lord, send your Holy Spirit into our lives, that we may be fully yours and images, icons, of you to this world. In Jesus' name we pray. Amen.

Dive **Deeper**

Speaking God's word can be hard. For inspiration and advice, watch Ascension's video "Fr. Mike on Evangelization: Telling the Story of God's Love" on Ascension Presents.

Reflect on the **Word**

- In Isaiah 44, we hear of Cyrus, who will be king of Persia in the distant future. At the end of this chapter, God says of Cyrus, "He is my shepherd, and he shall fulfil all my purpose" (Isaiah 44:28).

- In the beginning of Isaiah 43, the Lord warns his people that they will experience terrible things because they have turned away from him. But they are not to fear, because they are his. God tells them this before the Exile, so they are secure in knowing he has not abandoned them when it happens.

- God knows each of our stories. No matter what happens in our lives, we should not fear, because we are his.

- In Ezekiel 4 and 5, the prophet acts out a vision given to him by the Lord. He cuts off his hair and his beard with a sword and divides it into thirds. The first portion is burned up, representing fire, pestilence, or famine. The second is destroyed by the sword. The third is scattered to the winds and lost to history.

- Ezekiel is enacting in visual form what is happening to God's people because they rebelled against him.

- Even in allowing his people to experience such great suffering, the Lord is with them. He uses the pain of exile to bring them back to his heart.

- This is the consistent message of the prophets: Due to sin and rebellion, there will be suffering. It will seem like the Lord has abandoned his people, but he remains with them.

- Today might be the worst day of your life, but God is with you. After all, he says, "I have called you by name, you are mine" (Isaiah 43:1).

Take It to **Prayer**

Father in heaven, we give you praise. Thank you so much. Thank you for claiming us. Thank you for being with us even in the midst of our battles, in the midst of our trials, in the midst of our sufferings. You are with us every day, God, and we thank you. Please help us when we've turned away from you to allow you to bring us back. Help us to repent of our sins. Help us to trust in your love and in your grace. Especially, Lord, when we are confused, especially when we don't know where to turn, when we don't know what to do, help us to turn to you this day and every day. In Jesus' name we pray. Amen.

Dive **Deeper**

What is *the explanation of the human and cow dung in Ezekiel 4?*

In Ezekiel 4:12-13, the people of Israel are told by the prophet that they will bake their bread over unclean human dung. In Ezekiel's day, the custom would be to bake bread over a fire fueled with animal dung, the way it had been done for centuries. So why does God throw this curveball into the situation?

When Ezekiel speaks about the spiritual condition of Judah, he tells of an exile that will take the people from their own land to a foreign land filled with unclean food and strange customs. Here, the Lord is speaking to Judah symbolically to show them what the future holds—namely, they will be humbled because they have sinned against God by worshipping foreign gods. The reference to human dung is an expression to show just how bad Jerusalem has become.

(Interestingly, the recipe for bread as described in Ezekiel 4:9 has become the basis for the popular "Ezekiel Bread.")

–Jeff Cavins

Reflect on the **Word**

- Isaiah 44 proclaims that Cyrus, king of Persia, is God's shepherd. Though Cyrus worships false gods and does not know the Lord, he will be God's instrument in fulfilling his purpose. Cyrus will defeat the nations and return the people of Judah to Jerusalem—and Jerusalem will be rebuilt.

- Everything belongs to God. God can write with crooked lines.

- In Isaiah 45:9, we hear: "Woe to him who strives with his Maker, an earthen vessel with the potter! Does the clay say to him who fashions it, 'What are you making?'" Here, Isaiah proclaims the foolishness of treating God like our idol—treating God as if he is ours to command.

- Because they turn away from the Lord, his people suffer the sword, famine, pestilence, fire, and exile. But God says through Ezekiel, "Then they will know that I am the LORD" (Ezekiel 6:14). The things the people suffer are consequences of their decisions. These consequences do not mean God has abandoned them. The Lord has claimed them, and he wants them to return to him.

- God permits the Babylonians to destroy the Temple. Why does the Lord allow this? Because his people have desecrated the Temple with false worship.

- The prophet Ezekiel is a Levitical priest. In chapter 4, we see that Ezekiel is called to bear the iniquity of the people. Jesus, the great High Priest, carries the full weight of sinful humanity upon himself on the Cross.

- In our Baptism, we were anointed priest, prophet, and king in Jesus Christ. The Lord gives us the grace to fulfill this threefold office as his disciples.

Take It to **Prayer**

Father in heaven, we give you praise and glory. Thank you so much. Thank you for giving us your Word. Thank you for speaking to us. Thank you for showing your heart to us this day and every day. Thank you for bringing us to day 212. Lord God, I am so grateful for you and your love and your faithfulness, even when we are far from faithful, even when we are far from perfect. You just bring us back. You bring us back to pressing play. You bring us back to this opportunity to just simply listen to your Word proclaimed. Thank you so much. Thank you so much for not giving up on us and help us always to never, ever give up on you or your grace. Help us to hear your commands. Help us to hear your voice and say yes to you with all of our heart, mind, soul, and strength. In Jesus' name we pray. Amen.

Dive **Deeper**

POTTERY FROM THE TIME OF JESUS

Isaiah 45 uses the imagery of clay pottery to portray the humility that human beings should have before their Maker. St. Paul will do something similar in the New Testament. (See Romans 9.)

Reflect on the **Word**

- In Isaiah 48, the Lord addresses his people. Since they have been unfaithful to him, they will experience judgment. He laments in verse 18, "O that you had listened to my commandments! Then your peace would have been like a river, and your righteousness like the waves of the sea; your offspring would have been like the sand, and your descendants like its grains."

- Though the Lord will bring judgment because they have been unfaithful, he will restore his people if they turn back to him.

- In Ezekiel 8, though the prophet is in exile, the Lord gives him a vision of Jerusalem. He sees the Temple—both the abominations of false worship and the glory of God that still abides within it.

- The Lord repeatedly calls Ezekiel "son of man." In Daniel 7, this term will take on a new meaning as describing the one to whom God will hand all authority and power. Jesus will refer to himself as the Son of Man, claiming the promise of Daniel 7 to receive power, dominion, and glory from God.

- In Ezekiel 9, a man dressed in linen, which is a priestly garb, is told to put a mark on the foreheads of all those who mourn the abominations happening in the Temple. The mark is the Hebrew letter *tau*, which is the shape of a cross.

- Six men are sent to kill all of those who do not have a sign of a cross on their foreheads. In this foreshadowing, those who are mourning the loss of true worship in the Temple are marked with a cross on their foreheads, and this spares their lives.

- At Baptism, the priest (or deacon) and the parents and godparents make the Sign of the Cross on the child's forehead.

- Ezekiel 9, then, is a foreshadowing of the salvific work of Jesus, who will lay down his life by humbly submitting to death on the Cross.

Take It to **Prayer**

Father in heaven, we give you praise, and we give you glory, and we thank you so much for your Word. We thank you for the gift of life, and we thank you for the fact that things are alive, Lord God. Honestly, life is your gift. That we grow and we change is your gift. Both when we grow in strength and also when we grow in age and in weakness. Lord God, even in our infirmities you can make yourself known. Even in our weakness you can make your power known. And you do. You often choose to do that. So we give you permission to make yourself known to us and to the world in our weakness. We give you permission to make yourself known to us and to others around us in our brokenness and our woundedness. We make this prayer in the mighty name of Jesus Christ, our Lord. Amen.

Dive **Deeper**

Today, give the Lord permission to make himself known to you and to those around you, even in your woundedness and brokenness. Be attentive to the ways, whether big or small, God makes himself known in your day.

Reflect on the **Word**

- In Isaiah 49 and 50, we hear about the mission of a servant. The prophet here is referring to both the people of God and the coming Messiah.

- We see consolation when Isaiah proclaims, "The LORD called me from the womb, from the body of my mother he named my name. He made my mouth like a sharp sword" (Isaiah 49:1-2). He goes on, "You are my servant, Israel, in whom I will be glorified" (Isaiah 49:3). These are words of comfort that show that Israel will not be forgotten by the Lord.

- In Isaiah 49:14-15, God tells his people that even if a mother could forsake her child, God will not forget them. In verse 16, we hear that God has carved the names of his people on the palms of his hands—yet another way of saying that he will never forget us or stop loving us.

- After his resurrection, Jesus shows his apostles the wounds on his hands and feet. He allowed himself to be pierced for our sins; the marks on his hands and feet show his love for us.

- In Isaiah 50, we hear of the Suffering Servant. Jesus gave his back to those who struck him and did not cover his face from shame and spitting.

- In Ezekiel 11, due to the many abominations carried out in the Temple, the glory of the Lord departs for a time. But God does not abandon his people. In fact, the Lord's glory remains with them, though it is hidden during the Exile.

- In our own lives, the presence of God might seem hidden, but we know he is there.

Take It to **Prayer**

Father in heaven, we give you praise and thank you. Thank you so much, Lord. Thank you so much for prophesying not only the redemption of Israel, but the coming of Jesus Christ, your Servant, your Son, our Savior. We thank you so much, Lord God. We cannot even begin to praise your name for the faithfulness of the Jewish people, your covenant people; praise your name for the faithfulness of those first Christians, who were called by your Son, called by name. We thank you for the Christians throughout history who have been faithful and have endured storms and have endured trials and have passed on the Faith, down to us at this moment where we can read and we can listen to your Word. We thank you so much for all those who have gone before us. Thank you for our Jewish brothers and sisters. Thank you for our Christian brothers and sisters who have gone before us. We ask that you bring all people, all people, especially those who do not know you, those who do not know your Son, Jesus, into full covenant with you, God. Because you are the one who has been promised, and you are the one who has fulfilled that promise. Help us. Please help us all to hear your voice and to be drawn closer and closer to your heart. We make this prayer in Jesus' name. Amen.

Dive **Deeper**

Consider how God has carved your name in the palms of his hands and in the wounds of Jesus' crucifixion. If possible, spend some time in Eucharistic Adoration today to contemplate his love for you and how much you matter to him.

Reflect on the **Word**

- As always, in chapter 51 and 52, Isaiah preaches that judgment and destruction are coming but so is grace. There will be exile, but there will be a return from exile—and a future redeemer.

- The entire world—not just the people of Israel—will witness the humiliation, redemption, and exaltation of the Lord's servant, the Messiah. As Gentiles, we have been grafted on to the tree of the Lord's people; their story has become our story.

- In Ezekiel 12, the prophet himself is in exile, but he makes clear that the people's exile has not yet been completed, nor has the destruction of the Temple occurred. Due to ongoing abominations, Ezekiel says that what is coming will be even worse. The Lord's judgment is not far off.

- In chapter 13, Ezekiel says that there are many false prophets who tell the people what they want to hear, offering words of consolation when they should have offered words of condemnation. False prophets speak their own words, not the words of the Lord.

- We need to ask ourselves: Do we hear only what we want to hear? Do we only tell others what they want to hear? Do we hear and speak the words of God?

- To have a relationship with the Lord means that we must be willing to hear what we need to hear, see what we need to see, and do what we need to do. We can do this only with God's grace.

Take It to **Prayer**

Father in heaven, we give you praise, and we thank you so much. Thank you for your Word. We thank you for loving us. We thank you for calling us by name. We thank you for not only your justice but also for your mercy. And not only for your mercy but also for your justice. Because we can count on you, God. Because you are not fickle. You are not up and down. You are not hot or cold. You have said yes. And your yes has been declared for us. God, help us to declare our yes for you. Help us to be wise. Help us to be courageous. Help us above all things to be yours in all ways. In Jesus' name we pray. Amen.

Dive **Deeper**

A key distinction between true and false prophets is the source of their words. A false prophet speaks his own words, while a true prophet proclaims the words of the Lord. Thoughtfully consider your own speech today and discern whether you are hearing and speaking God's words or your own.

Reflect on the **Word**

- Isaiah 53 brings us back to the prophecy of the Suffering Servant: "He was despised and rejected by men; a man of sorrows, and acquainted with grief" (Isaiah 53:3). Jesus will embody these words more than six hundred years after the prophet writes them.

- In Isaiah 54, we see mercy and comfort offered. While we should rightly acknowledge our guilt for our sins, we should not be afraid to seek the Lord's mercy and forgiveness.

- Remember that Ezekiel is writing among those who are already exiled in Babylon. His visions show that those who still remain in Jerusalem have not turned back to God. So the Lord's glory will depart from the Temple. Yet, despite this, Ezekiel 11:19-20 offers a promise: "I will give them one heart, and put a new spirit within them; I will take the stony heart out of their flesh and give them a heart of flesh, that they may walk in my statutes and keep my ordinances and obey them; and they shall be my people, and I will be their God."

- God tolerates no rivals to him in our hearts. Similarly, though we can have many friends, we can only have one spouse. Family is important, and things like work are also important, but nothing can take the place of God in our lives.

- In Ezekiel 15, we see the analogy of the vine that is used for nothing. The Lord chose Israel not because they were wiser or more beautiful or more powerful than all the nations. He chose them precisely because they were small and needed him to make them glorious—and bring his salvation to the world. If they turn away from him, though, they become useless.

- We need to pursue righteousness and a right relationship with the Lord, but we need to pray that the people around us do so as well. We need to intercede on their behalf that their lives might be changed by a relationship with God.

Take It to **Prayer**

Father in heaven, we give you praise and thank you so much. God, thank you for this opportunity to be close to you and close to your Word. Thank you so much for your promise of a Messiah, who is willing to suffer for us, and did and has suffered for us. Thank you for the deliverance of not only the people of Israel in sending your Son, our Lord God, Jesus Christ. But also, thank you for sending him for us. Many of us were not your Chosen People, until you have chosen us in Jesus. And so we just give you thanks, and we give you praise, and we ask that you please hear our prayers and receive our thanks, receive our praise this day and every day. In Jesus' name we pray. Amen.

Dive **Deeper**

Intercede on behalf of those in your life today. Pray for their particular intentions and situations, and pray that they would choose God in those situations.

Reflect on the **Word**

- Today, we hear of God's promise to all: "Come receive bread without payment." In Isaiah 56, we hear that strangers are brought into the covenant.

- To everyone who worships the Lord as he desires, loves his name, keeps the Sabbath, and holds fast to the covenant, the Lord says, "These I will bring to my holy mountain, and make them joyful in my house of prayer; their burnt offerings and their sacrifices will be accepted on my altar" (Isaiah 56:7).

- As Isaiah 55:8-9 proclaims, "For my thoughts are not your thoughts, neither are your ways my ways, says the LORD. For as the heavens are higher than the earth, so are my ways higher than your ways and my thoughts than your thoughts." If we let our view of the world be shaped by the Word of God, then we begin to see things as God sees them. We begin to love as God loves.

- In Isaiah 55:11, we hear the promise of God regarding the power of his Word: "It shall not return to me empty, but it shall accomplish that which I intend, and prosper in the thing for which I sent it."

- In Ezekiel 16, we again hear the story of Israel, who is represented by a newborn whom no one wanted. Israel is claimed by God and nurtured.

- Through Ezekiel, God uses the image of a woman whom he clothes with beauty and grace, fine linen and jewelry. But she becomes captivated by her own beauty. Though God makes her his, she squanders this relationship and pursues other lovers. Her adultery is an image for idolatry.

- We can make idols of the blessings God has given us. But our idols end up giving us nothing. Only the true God can love us.

- At the end of Ezekiel 16, God proclaims that he will establish an everlasting covenant with his people. We see this reality expressed by Jesus at the Last Supper, when he says to his apostles, "This chalice which is poured out for you is the new covenant in my blood" (Luke 22:20).

- Jesus has given us the house of prayer for all nations—the Church—which brings all into a saving covenant relationship with the Lord.

Take It to **Prayer**

Father in heaven, we give you praise and glory. Every single day you bring us to this place where we get to hear your Word. And your Word ... just like Isaiah described, your Word is living and effective. Your Word does not return to you void. Your Word accomplishes your will. And we are just so grateful. Your Word accomplishes your will, Lord God, just as the rain and snow come down. So please help us. Help us to say yes to what you will for us. Help us to say yes to your Word today for us. And help us to say yes to you and your will for us this day and every day. In Jesus' name we pray. Amen.

Dive **Deeper**

Throughout the course of reading the Bible this year, how has your view of the world been shaped by the Word of God? Think of how the ways you see the world and love others have been changed for the better and praise the Lord for it.

Reflect on the **Word**

- Remember, in Ezekiel 16, idolatry is represented as adultery. Like the people of Israel, we are broken and turn away from the God who loves us to pursue created things. This is the essence of idolatry.

- In Isaiah 57, the image of adultery is used to condemn idolatry. The people were making offerings to false gods. There is even reference to worship of Molech, to whom children were sacrificed in the ancient days.

- In Isaiah 58, we see the distinction between true and false worship, proper and improper fasting. The people worship falsely, then ask why the Lord does not hear them. God responds that they are seeking their own pleasure with this type of fasting, which will prevent their prayers from being heard.

- Ultimately, our motive for praying and reading the Bible is to grow in a true relationship with God.

- Jesus honors the Sabbath by performing miracles and setting people free. This enrages the Pharisees, who are focused entirely on what is described in the last part of Isaiah 58 about keeping the Sabbath day holy. They forget the first part about letting the oppressed go free. So Jesus is being faithful to the heart of the entire Law.

- Ezekiel 18 talks about God's justice and how each of us is judged by our own conduct. Each of us has to choose to be faithful—or unfaithful—to the Lord.

Take It to **Prayer**

Father in heaven, we give you praise, and we thank you. We thank you so much for giving us your wisdom and sharing with us the way in which you see, the way in which you think. Just like we recognize yesterday that you spoke to us and said that your ways are not our ways. Our minds, our thoughts, are not your thoughts. We are so grateful for that. We are so grateful that you do share your ways. You share your thoughts with us. And so we ask you to please, once again, like we prayed yesterday, like we keep on praying, allow your words to continue to change our hearts. Allow your power to change our lives. Allow your grace to change us forever, so we can belong to you not only today but also in eternity. In Jesus' name we pray. Amen.

Dive **Deeper**

We read earlier that God would punish subsequent generations for the sins of their fathers. Is this not true after Ezekiel's time?

Ezekiel 18 stresses that each person will be judged according to his or her own sins, not the sins of his or her parents or children. How does this square with the fact that the Israelites were actually punished with exile because of their fathers' disobedience?

Here, we need to make a distinction. In this world, all of us suffer due to the sins of others, at least indirectly. Ezekiel says that if someone is righteous during the time of exile and keeps the commandments of the Lord, then he or she will be rewarded by the Lord in the next life. Those who are wicked and do not keep the commandments of the Lord will be punished.

When we are judged at the end of our lives, we will be judged for our own actions, not those of others. We should remember that we will not be saved because our parents were faithful to God; we will be saved if *we* are faithful to him.

-Kara Logan

Reflect on the **Word**

- Proverbs 13:11 offers us some practical advice: "Wealth hastily gotten will dwindle, but he who gathers little by little will increase it." We need to increase in wealth—and wisdom—a little every day.

- At the beginning of chapter 59, Isaiah makes it clear that when we think the Lord is not listening to us, it is our sins that separate us. In verse 10, he says we grope like the blind, because the Lord has taken away his light.

- Isaiah 60:1 offers hope that the light will shine if we repent and turn back to the Lord: "Arise, shine; for your light has come, and the glory of the LORD has risen upon you."

- Jesus tells his disciples that they are the salt of the earth and the light of the world (see Matthew 5:13-16). We must not put the light of Christ under a basket but need to let it shine in a dark world. People need to see what Jesus has done in our lives so they can be inspired to follow him.

- In Ezekiel 19, there is a lamentation about a lioness and her young cubs. The lioness represents the tribe of Judah. The lions born to her are the kings of Judah who are conquered. The first lion mentioned is Jehoahaz, son of King Josiah, whose reign is evil and lasts only a few months. He is taken prisoner to Egypt. The next lion is the next king, Jehoiakim. Another bad king, he reigns for eleven years but is taken away in chains by the king of Babylon. (See 2 Chronicles 36:1-6.)

- The lamentation about the vine might refer to King Zedekiah. Zedekiah is the last of the kings of the line of David. From Zedekiah until Jesus, the royal line of David goes "underground." This is why Ezekiel is offering this lament, for he knows of the promise made to David that his dynasty will not end and a descendant of his will come to the throne.

- For centuries, the people of Israel wonder how God will fulfill his promise of an everlasting kingdom rooted in the line of David.

- We too can find ourselves walking in darkness. Yet we know that if we hold on to our Father's hand, he will lead us to the place of light.

Take It to **Prayer**

Father in heaven, we give you praise and glory. We thank you so much for your Word. And we thank you for giving us your presence and your wisdom. Help us to receive your wisdom and not to just let it pass us by but to live it. To base our lives upon you and upon the truth that you impart and the wisdom that you share with us. In Jesus' name we pray. Amen.

Dive **Deeper**

A VINEYARD IN THE HOLY LAND

This image shows part of a vineyard owned by the Trappist monastery in Latrun, Israel. Ezekiel 19 compares Israel to a vine, once flourishing and fruitful, now plucked and burned.

Reflect on the **Word**

- Isaiah 61 opens with the words, "The Spirit of the Lord GOD is upon me, because the LORD has anointed me to bring good tidings to the afflicted; he has sent me to bind up the brokenhearted, to proclaim liberty to the captives, and the opening of the prison to those who are bound; to proclaim the year of the LORD's favor, and the day of vengeance of our God." In Luke, we see that Jesus enters the synagogue and reads these very words from Isaiah, saying, "Today this Scripture has been fulfilled in your hearing" (Luke 4:21).

- Isaiah 61 proclaims that the Lord hates evil and loves goodness—and he will establish an everlasting covenant. Jesus fulfills this promise.

- Isaiah 62 says that, despite destruction and exile, the Lord promises that his people will not be forsaken. One day, we will rejoice.

- In Ezekiel 20, we see a synopsis of all the places God's people have been unfaithful, rejected his statutes, and profaned the Sabbath by going after idols.

- Sabbath, *Shabbat* in Hebrew, is the seventh day of the week, Saturday. The Lord says, "I gave them my sabbaths, as a sign between me and them" (Ezekiel 20:12). A covenant establishes a relationship, and the sign of God's covenant relationship is this dedicated time to worship him.

- The two primary tasks of the Sabbath are worship and rest. Worshipping means living as someone who belongs to the Lord, and resting shows one is free and not in bondage. Throughout the Bible, there is much said about the importance of faithfully keeping the Sabbath.

- Sunday, the day of the Lord's resurrection, is the new Sabbath. For Christians, the sign of the covenant for us is to worship and to rest every Sunday. Do we treat Sunday as a day set apart, where we rest and worship the Lord?

- Sometimes, this rest can involve family and friends. There are many people who are alone on weekends, and they go to church by themselves, sit and pray by themselves, and go home by themselves. If that's you, know that the prayers of this community are with you, because you are not alone.

Take It to **Prayer**

Father in heaven, we give you praise and glory. We thank you so much for this day. Thank you for your Word. Thank you for this opportunity to be together. Thank you for constantly calling us back to yourself. Thank you, Lord, for your word in Isaiah of promise, your word in Isaiah of consolation, your word in Isaiah of, yes, destruction and horrible things have to happen, but it is all so that we can come back to you and you can bless us. So help us come back to you and please bless us this day. Especially bless the members of this community, God, who stand in particular need of your help right now. Who stand in particular need of our prayers. Who stand in particular need of your grace. Give them your grace this day and every day. In Jesus' name we pray. Amen.

Dive **Deeper**

As a Christian, how do you observe Sunday as a day of worship and rest? Consider some ways you can make your observance of Sundays more spiritually fruitful.

Reflect on the **Word**

- As Proverbs 13:20 tells us, "He who walks with wise men becomes wise, but the companion of fools will suffer harm." We become wise when we associate with wise people, and we become holy when we are around holy people.

- If we intentionally surround ourselves with people who are indifferent to God and to the plight of those around us, then we can become indifferent as well.

- Today, Isaiah 63:6 speaks of God's just vengeance, while verse 7 speaks of his merciful love. We recognize that God's justice and mercy are not opposed. We deserve God's justice, but we are freely given his mercy.

- Ezekiel lays out the sins of Jerusalem, including treating one's neighbor unjustly, not caring for the poor, violating the Sabbath, and treating holy things as common. While true religion involves worship of God, it also involves caring for the poor, the widow, the orphan, and all those who need help.

- So God's people are neither worshipping him correctly nor showing mercy to others.

- In chapter 22, the Lord says that he is looking for someone willing to stand up and intercede for the people. No one will do so.

- Each of us should ask ourselves: Do we regularly go before the Lord and intercede for those we love and for those who have asked us to pray for them? Praying to the Lord on behalf of others shows mercy, can change their hearts, and can bring them into a deeper relationship with the Lord.

Take It to **Prayer**

Father in heaven, we give you praise, and we thank you so much. We thank you and give you love. That's all. Just thank you today. Thank you for bringing us to this day. We know that you are good. We know that you are God. We know that you love us and so there's nothing else to say but thank you for who you are. Thank you for all that you've done. Thank you for being with us and never abandoning us. Help us to walk with you. Bring people into our lives who can walk with us so that we can be the men and women that you have called us to be this day and every day. In Jesus' name we pray. Amen.

Dive **Deeper**

What are some tips *for reading the prophets?*

The prophets of the Old Testament wrote in a time and to a culture very different from our own, using concepts and language that are foreign to our modern understanding. In general, a prophet's message was intended to proclaim God's word to the people—and exhort them to hear and obey it. In some cases, the prophetic message is obvious, but many times it is veiled in symbolic language that can only be understood in the context of the whole of the Bible.

Here are a few tips to help read the prophets: (1) Learn to whom the prophet is proclaiming his message—e.g., the united kingdom of the Israelites, the divided kingdom, or humanity as a whole. (2) Find out how the particular group the prophet is addressing has been unfaithful to the Lord. (3) Note the prophet's message regarding the present and future consequences of their disobedience to God. (4) Learn the ways God, through this prophet, seeks to draw the people back to himself. (5) Though the prophets spoke to ancient peoples, see how each prophet's message applies to us as Christians. (6) Prayerfully discern how Jesus fulfills the prophet's message. Remember, the entire Bible is directed to the coming of the Messiah.

–Jeff Cavins

Reflect on the **Word**

- Through his prophets, the Lord seeks to bring his people back to him.

- In Proverbs 13:24, we see a challenging word about discipline: "He who spares the rod hates his son." Of course, this is not advocating physical abuse but rather loving discipline. If we love our children, like God, we sometimes need to punish them to keep them on the right path.

- Ezekiel draws a metaphor with two women named Oholah, who represents Samaria and Israel, and Oholibah, who represents Judah. Though they come from Egypt, both "play the harlot" with Assyria. Again, we see the metaphor of adultery. God's people are his, and he will not tolerate rivals. It is like a spousal relationship. Ezekiel 23 offers a graphic description of how his people have turned away from the Lord God and are giving themselves over to false gods.

- We see in chapter 24 that Ezekiel's wife dies. The Lord tells him that his heart will be pierced, but he will not mourn. People will wonder why he is not mourning the loss of his wife.

- Here, Ezekiel might be drawing a parallel to the loss of the Temple. It will be destroyed, and yet the people will not mourn its destruction, as if they do not care.

- How often are we indifferent to the blasphemy we see? How indifferent are we sometimes to those who walk away from the Lord?

Take It to **Prayer**

Father in heaven, we thank you so much, and we give you praise. Lord God, thank you for this day. And thank you for continuing to call us back. We get off course so easily, Lord God. But you are just so gentle with us in bringing us back often. Sometimes you're not. Sometimes we need to be woken up. And sometimes you shout to us to wake us up, and we thank you for that. We thank you for your gentleness. We also thank you for your strength. We thank you that you are desperate, in some ways you are so desperate, Lord, to bring us back to your heart. So please today do whatever it takes. Do whatever it takes to bring us back to your heart today, Lord God, whether that be a gentle call, or a gentle correction, or whether that be something big, Lord God. Do whatever it takes to get us back to your heart this day so we can live our eternity and this day—so we can live this day and our eternity with you forever. In Jesus' name we pray. Amen.

Dive **Deeper**

Prayerfully consider the following questions:
How often am I indifferent to the blasphemy I see?
Am I indifferent to those who walk away from the Lord?

Reflect on the **Word**

- Ezekiel preaches about how wrong it is for God's people to be indifferent to the destruction of the Temple.

- The end of Isaiah speaks of the day when all will rejoice with Jerusalem. In Isaiah 66, we hear that all who mourned over her will now rejoice with her. The Lord "will extend prosperity to her like a river, and the wealth of the nations like an overflowing stream" (Isaiah 66:12).

- Isaiah uses the term "the new heavens and the new earth" (Isaiah 6:22).

- God's promises to Abraham were land, dynasty, and worldwide blessing. Isaiah concludes this book talking about all who will come, journeying from afar, to worship the Messiah.

- Not only will the Lord restore his blessing to the Jewish people, but he is also going to extend his goodness and glory to all the nations. As Isaiah 66:23 says, "All flesh shall come to worship."

- There are ministerial priests in the New Covenant, and every baptized Christian shares in the priesthood of Jesus Christ.

Take It to **Prayer**

Father in heaven, we give you praise, and we thank you so much. Lord, thank you for journeying with us. Lord, I know that the book of the prophet Isaiah can be so intimidating. The books of any of the major prophets can be so intimidating. Here we are in the middle of Ezekiel. Here we are concluding Isaiah. And yet you walked with us and held our hands as we just sought to understand what it was that you were speaking to the people of Jerusalem, the people of Israel, at the time and what you are speaking to us today. Lord God, as often as your Word is confusing, and as often as your Word ... we only understand it as through a veil darkly ... we ask that you please continue to illuminate our minds. And above all, even when our minds are darkened, to inflame our hearts with a love for you that we can have the appropriate approach to you, the appropriate attitude toward you, the appropriate response to you. We ask that you match our emotions up with reality around us. That we only feel fear when there is something to fear. That we feel joy when there is something to be joyful at. We mourn those things we are called upon to mourn. We grieve when we are called upon to grieve. And we rejoice when we are called upon to rejoice. Lord God, knit us back together. Make us whole again. In Jesus' name we pray. Amen.

Dive **Deeper**

Today, pray that the Lord will help you respond to him with love and trust even when his Word is difficult to understand.

Reflect on the **Word**

- Like Ezekiel, Jeremiah is also a priest. Jeremiah spends most of his life and prophetic ministry in Judah.

- Jeremiah is known as the "weeping prophet." He has a sensitive heart for the people, and his heart is sensitive to the Lord. At the beginning of his prophetic ministry, God tells Jeremiah that the people will not listen to him.

- The Lord's call to Jeremiah is awe-inspiring: "Before I formed you in the womb I knew you, and before you were born I consecrated you; I appointed you a prophet to the nations" (Jeremiah 1:5).

- God knows each of us, before we are even formed in our mother's womb—and he gives each of us a call in our lives. Like Jeremiah, God commissions each of us for a particular task, and people might not listen to us, either.

- Though reluctant at first, Jeremiah fully accepts God's call, even though it will cost him to obey. Jeremiah is a great example for us. Belonging to the Lord means that we are willing to do what he asks of us, no matter what.

- While Ezekiel is married, Jeremiah is not. Some commentators suggest that Jeremiah's life is marked by so much pain that the Lord spares any woman from having to experience this suffering as his wife.

- Jeremiah is called to intimacy with God alone as he walks through the world.

- There are people all around us who also walk alone, although they are known and loved by God. Pray that we keep our eyes open to recognize these people, that we might walk beside them and love them.

Take It to **Prayer**

Father in heaven, we thank you and give you praise. Lord, thank you so much. Thank you for this day and thank you for your words of conviction, even your words of condemnation because, Lord God, we never want to be on the receiving end of those words. We never want to be on the receiving end of your judgment, of your justice. God, we deserve your justice, but we need your mercy. And so when we hear your words to the city of Tyre, and we hear what you are going to do with Jeremiah's life, we give you thanks that you spoke these words and you revealed your longing for justice and the fact that you are a God of justice and you do not delay in your judgment. Lord God, in the way that you do not delay in your judgment, please also do not delay in your mercy. Those of us ... we have failed you and have fallen, and we need your mercy more than ever right now in this moment in our lives. This moment in my life, I just ask you for your mercy today, Lord. Your mercy is new every morning. Help me to turn back to you. Help us all to turn back to you in whatever way, great or small, that we have wandered away or fallen away or run away. Help us always to find the way back to you in Jesus. We make this prayer in the name of Jesus. Amen.

Dive **Deeper**

Today, pay special attention to the people around you who may be walking alone. Pray for them and let them know they are known and loved through your words or actions.

Reflect on the **Word**

- Proverbs 14:12 reminds us that we should never choose our plan over God's will.

- In Ezekiel 28, the prophet speaks of the downfall of Tyre and Sidon. These are wealthy port cities on the Mediterranean Sea. Ezekiel laments over Tyre, describing how it has been overcome by pride. When God gives us wisdom, beauty, or wealth, we can sometimes begin to think these are our right and become proud.

- In Ezekiel 28, the Lord says that he did not raise Israel up for its own sake but to show his holiness. Likewise, our lives belong to God and should manifest his holiness to those around us.

- Jeremiah preaches for roughly fifty years. He speaks harsh words out of great love.

- In Jeremiah 2, we see some of the deeds that break the prophet's heart—apostasy, idolatry, and adultery among God's people. The Lord tells Jeremiah to tell his people that he remembers when they used to be faithful, as a husband might say to his wife, "I remember when you used to look at me like you loved me."

- In Jeremiah 2:5, the Lord asks his people why they have turned away from him. Then in verse 13, God says, "For my people have committed two evils: they have forsaken me, the fountain of living waters, and hewed out cisterns for themselves, broken cisterns, that can hold no water"—that is, they have sought to worship idols rather than him.

- In Jeremiah 2:26, we hear, "As a thief is shamed when caught, so the house of Israel shall be shamed." Thieves are not ashamed when they steal but only when they are caught. Similarly, many times we are not ashamed when we sin but only when we are caught sinning.

- God speaks to us today and calls us back to him. We need his grace.

Take It to **Prayer**

Father in heaven, we give you praise, and we thank you so much. We thank you, as every day that we pray, we thank you for your Word. We thank you for revealing to us your call to repent, your call to come back to you. We thank you for revealing to us the fact that you have a plan for our lives and that you actually want us to be blessed by you. You want us to be close to you. You want us to be as faithful to you as you are to us. And even when we are not faithful, even when we fail, you have not abandoned us. Because you are a good Dad. And so, Father, today—Dad, today—we thank you. We thank you for your gift. Thank you for your wisdom. And thank you for never abandoning us and continuing to call us back to your heart. Help us to say yes to your heart. Help us to say yes to your will. And help us to turn away from what we have turned to in place of you. What we have placed our trust in, in place of you. What we have given our heart to instead of you. In Jesus' name we pray. Amen.

Dive **Deeper**

It can be hard to let go of our will and embrace God's plan for us. View Fr. Mike's video "When Your Desires and God's Plans Are Different" on Ascension Presents.

Reflect on the **Word**

- Sometimes we think having boundaries in our lives limits freedom. Proverbs 14:16 reminds us of the difference between *license*—getting to do whatever I want—and *freedom*—the power to do what I ought.

- Interior freedom allows us to love and worship in the way God calls us. If we do not love like we should, this is because we do not have interior freedom.

- To be able to turn away from evil when we see it is a great gift.

- In Ezekiel 30, the prophet warns the people against making an alliance with Egypt. Through these prophesies of Ezekiel, we see how God uses pagan nations, such as Babylon, to correct his people. The Lord uses flawed, even evil, people to bring about his plan of salvation.

- In the days of King Josiah, some exchanged Temple worship of God for idolatry. "Every high hill and under every green tree" (Jeremiah 3:6) were places where idol worship and ritual immorality were practiced.

- Jeremiah accuses the people of teaching others to sin through scandal—that is, leading others to sin by one's sinful example.

- The effect of our sins is not confined to us. Our sins affect those around us, who often have to suffer for them as well.

Take It to **Prayer**

Father in heaven, we give you praise. We thank you once again for this day. We thank you for speaking to us. We thank you for calling us to be yours. We thank you for giving us the grace to turn to you every day once again. Please receive our thanks. Receive our praise this day. And help us to walk in your ways. Help us to be wise. Help us to not be foolish, but to be prudent and to use the gifts you have given us well. Especially the gift of this day. In Jesus' name we pray. Amen.

Dive **Deeper**

THE NILE RIVER

This image shows the shoreline of the Nile River in Egypt. Contrary to the Pharaoh's words, God alone created the world and has dominion over the created order. (See Ezekiel 29.)

Reflect on the **Word**

- In Ezekiel 31 and 32, we see an extension of the prophecy against Pharaoh. Here, Ezekiel is not only speaking to the king of Egypt but also to the people of God.

- Ezekiel tells the people of Judah and Jerusalem what will happen to the nation in which they placed their trust: Egypt (spoken of as a great cedar tree) will collapse. They should have trusted in God.

- Jeremiah begins his preaching before Jerusalem is destroyed. Though he continues to preach repentance, he knows that this destruction will come.

- We can see the prophet's sorrow in Jeremiah 4:19—"My anguish, my anguish! I writhe in pain! Oh, the walls of my heart! My heart is beating wildly; I cannot keep silent; for I hear the sound of the trumpet, the alarm of war."

- Jeremiah preaches repentance, telling the people to prepare themselves for the coming judgment of the Lord. He says that God's people are foolish, lacking in understanding. They are skilled in doing evil but do not know how to do good.

- It is the same today. We can become very skilled at committing sin. We need to ask God to help us come back to him when we fall and teach us how to do good.

- Just as in Jeremiah's day, life can go from being "fine" to "not fine" suddenly. We need to ask God to help us to become wise in virtue in preparation for that day.

Take It to **Prayer**

Father in heaven, we give you praise and glory. We thank you so much. Lord God, what a gift you are, and what a gift your Word is. What an incredible gift it is to be able to be on day 227 on this journey through your Word and the journey of your Word through us. Because that is what's happening, Lord God. It's not just our journeying through your Word. It is your story, your Word, your self journeying through us, making your way to our minds, to our hearts, and to our actions that our lives may be built upon your truth and your wisdom. Lord God, help us to put that truth and wisdom into practice this day and every day. Help us to build our lives upon you, upon Jesus Christ, the Rock. Help us to be inspired and guided and given courage by the Holy Spirit at every moment of every day all of our lives. In Jesus' name we pray. Amen.

Dive **Deeper**

One of the defining characteristics of a person striving for holiness is a commitment to return to God even after a fall. Today, contemplate the open arms of the Lord. Ask him to help you become skilled at learning how to come back to him.

Reflect on the **Word**

- Ezekiel 33 is a pivot point of the Scripture—when the destruction of Jerusalem occurs.

- At the beginning of Ezekiel 33, the obligations of a watchman are described. If he fails to warn the people of an impending attack, he will be responsible for his failure. The Lord tells Ezekiel that he is the watchman for the Israelites.

- The role of the prophet is to speak whatever God wants spoken. He is not responsible if the people refuse to listen and obey the Lord's words.

- In James 3, the apostle warns that not many should aspire to be teachers because they will face a stricter judgment. Priests, prophets, and teachers all have a great responsibility to teach the truth. We proclaim the truth not only with our words but by our actions.

- The Lord tells Ezekiel at the end of chapter 33 that the people will hear his message but will not allow themselves to be changed by it.

- In the time of Jeremiah, there are false prophets who are popular because they speak what the people want to hear. Jeremiah, though, is rejected because he speaks what people need to hear—the Word of the Lord. Likewise, we must be on guard against false prophets in our own day.

- Jeremiah 5:4-5 speaks of the coming judgment of the Lord. The prophet calls the people to repent, but neither the great nor the poor do so. "Breaking the yoke" is a phrase signifying rebellion against the Lord. Each of us can be rebellious, and we are called to submit ourselves to God and his will.

- God draws our attention to our need to be converted—not just in our actions but in the depths of our hearts.

Take It to **Prayer**

Father in heaven, we give you praise and glory. Lord God, thank you for continuing to put before us wisdom as a goal. And not just wisdom as the end, but wisdom as the goal to have so that we can have you as our end—that you can be the one thing that our hearts are set upon. Lord God, in all the stuff that we have to do, in all the people we have to love, in all the things that we care about in our lives, they are gifts. And yet they can oftentimes take our eyes off of you, off of the Giver. So please, Lord God, help us to have our eyes fixed on you. To have our hearts fixed on you. To have all of our desires fixed on you so much that we desire nothing more than to live wisely so that we can attain you, that we can have you as the source and center of our lives. In Jesus' name we pray. Amen.

Dive **Deeper**

Like Jeremiah, we are called to speak the truth even when it is difficult. Today, turn to the appendix on page 257 to learn about some ways to speak the truth at all times.

Reflect on the **Word**

- Jeremiah 6, Ezekiel 34, and Proverbs 14 are all focused on leadership. In Proverbs 14 we are reminded that the role of a king is to be the person who has been entrusted with the people of God. In Ezekiel 34, God rebukes the shepherds of Israel who have not cared for the sheep but only themselves.

- Every year priests will read from St. Augustine, who reminds them that in the new covenant they have become the shepherds of the people.

- While Jesus is the Good Shepherd who cares for his sheep, here we can also reflect on our own lives to see if we are only taking care of ourselves or if we are giving of ourselves for others.

- Ezekiel 34:11 offers words of consolation. The Lord is a shepherd who will go out, seek his lost sheep, and bring them home to their own land. While the prophet is speaking here of the people of Israel, he also anticipates the coming of Jesus, the Good Shepherd.

- In Jeremiah 6:14, we hear that the leaders of Israel do not actually seek to heal the wounds of the people but merely offer words of consolation. Those who have been given authority must truly live for others, not themselves.

- False prophets proclaim that peace is coming, but there is no peace. It requires courage to speak the truth, especially when the truth is unpopular.

- In Jeremiah 6:15, we are told that the people no longer feel shame for their misdeeds.

- The people's lack of shame means that they have forgotten the goodness of their hearts. When we feel ashamed by our sins, we should recognize we feel this because something good in us has been wounded.

Take It to **Prayer**

Father in heaven, we give you praise and glory. We thank you so much. These prophets have just called us, called me, to repentance and called me to just want to belong to you with everything I am, with everything we are. Help us. Help us to please turn to you completely, to belong to you fully, to be yours now and forever. We make this prayer in the mighty name of Jesus Christ, our Lord. Amen.

Dive **Deeper**

SHEPHERD WATCHING HIS FLOCK

In Ezekiel 34, God is presented as the shepherd who will personally protect and guide Israel. In this photograph, a modern-day shepherd accompanies his flock.

Reflect on the **Word**

- The Israelites know they have been chosen by the Lord and that he dwells in the Temple. In their pride, they believe that God will remain with them regardless of their actions.

- In Jeremiah 7:12, the Lord tells the people to go to Shiloh, a place where sacrifices were once offered but no longer are. Here, God reminds them that he has removed his presence from a sacred place in the past.

- In Matthew 16, Jesus proclaims the establishment of his Church, built upon Peter, the rock. Yet many of us who acknowledge the Church fail to live faithfully within it.

- Similarly, in John 6, Jesus makes it clear that the Eucharist is his Body, Blood, Soul, and Divinity. Though we might receive Jesus in Holy Communion, we still might fail to conform our lives fully to him.

- We hear today the advice "follow your heart." But our hearts can lead us astray. The first two movements of conversion are distrust of self and trust in the Lord. I do not know what is good for me, but I can trust God does.

- False worship often led to the valley of Hinnom (Gehenna), where people would offer their children as burnt offerings to worship a false god.

- While Jeremiah prophecies before the destruction of Jerusalem, Ezekiel preaches after that destruction has occurred. So, in Ezekiel 36:8, we hear words of hope spoken to a people already in exile—words of hope of return.

- Through Ezekiel, the Lord proclaims that he will transform the people's hearts of stone into hearts of flesh.

Take It to **Prayer**

Father in heaven, we give you praise, and we give you glory. We thank you so much every day for your Word, every day for your faithfulness to us, and also for you reminding us not only of our need to be faithful to you, but to be attentive to the people around us. Lord God, in Jeremiah you highlight how your people failed to take care of the needy, the poor, the orphaned, those without fathers, without mothers. And here in the book of Proverbs you also note that those who oppress a poor man insult our Maker: and then we insult you. But he who is kind to the needy honors the Lord. And Lord God, we want to be those kinds of people that are not blind to the needs of the people around us, not deaf to the cries of the poor, but take the time to see, to note, and to act. Help us to never be false children to you. Help us to always be children who are like you not only in our thoughts and speech but also in our actions. Help us to be your image in this world. In Jesus' name we pray. Amen.

Dive **Deeper**

The Litany of Trust is a beautiful prayer by the Sisters of Life to grow in trust. Pray it today and ask the Lord to give you a new heart, one that fully trusts in him!

Reflect on the **Word**

- In Jeremiah 8, the prophet tells the people to brace themselves for the destruction of Jerusalem, describing how the bones of its priests, prophets, and inhabitants will be brought out.

- Since God's people have gone after foreign gods of foreign peoples, they will now be exiled to a foreign land. They will be surrounded and enslaved by the idolatry they sought.

- When we belong to the Lord, we are not his slaves—we are his sons and daughters. Yet, we too can give our hearts to false gods that promise everything and deliver nothing.

- Ezekiel 37 presents the prophet's vision of the valley of the dry bones. The Lord tells Ezekiel to speak his words over the dry bones, which then become alive and stand up. Here, the Lord is telling his exiled people that he will one day give them his Spirit and that they will return to their own land. God has used Babylon not to destroy his people but to call them back to him.

- We are also presented with an image of two sticks—representing Judah and Israel—which Ezekiel holds together to represent how God will unify his people.

- In Ezekiel 37, the Lord promises a future king in the line of David, the Messiah, who will be the sole shepherd of one people and one kingdom. In his Gospel, Matthew shows how Jesus is the fulfillment of this promise.

- Jesus Christ will bring all peoples to himself—and will bring the kingdom of Israel to its fulfillment in his Church.

Take It to **Prayer**

Father in heaven, we give you praise and glory. You are good. You are our Father. You are our Dad. We thank you so much. And God, you have made your heart known to us, and you have called us back to yourself. You, who can raise the dead to life. You, who conquered death so that death does not have power to conquer us. We ask you to send that Spirit, the Spirit that came upon the dry bones as Ezekiel prophesied, the Spirit that raised Jesus Christ from the dead, the Spirit that you gave to the Apostles and you give to us, your children, now. We ask for that Holy Spirit to bring us to life, especially, Lord, the broken parts of us, the dead parts of us, the parts that seem lost and without hope, the parts of us that disqualify us, or we believe that they disqualify us. Lord God, let your Holy Spirit come upon us and those parts. Bring us to life. Bring us to you. Bring us home. We ask this in Jesus' name. Amen.

Dive **Deeper**

Why is David held up in the Scriptures as a positive example? He made many mistakes.

The Bible describes David as "a man after God's own heart" (see 1 Samuel 13:14). He trusts in the Lord, relying on the Lord when he battles Goliath, for example (see 1 Samuel 17). When David sins with Bathsheba and later has her husband killed, he acknowledges his sin, repents, and asks God to forgive him (see Psalm 51). Throughout David's reign, although he seemingly fails as a father, he is humble and receives the mercy of God.

We see through the prophets that the Israelites are waiting with great hope for a "new David" when the twelve tribes will be under one king again. God promises David in 2 Samuel 7:13 that one of his offspring will be on the throne forever, a promise repeated in Ezekiel 37. This promise is ultimately fulfilled in Jesus Christ. The kingdom of David is thus a type, though imperfect, of the everlasting kingdom, the Church. And David is a type, though imperfect, of the Messiah, the King of Kings, Jesus Christ.

–Kara Logan

Reflect on the **Word**

- In Jeremiah 9, we see that the injustice surrounding the prophet does not just make him angry—it breaks his heart.

- Jeremiah speaks of how the people have grown accustomed to falsehood and cannot be trusted. When someone has shown that he or she is not trustworthy, then we need to be wary of that person. People who are not true to their promises to the Lord will not be true to their promises to others.

- In Jeremiah 9:23-24, the prophet reminds us not to put our trust in our wisdom, might, or riches. Instead, we should find glory in knowing the Lord.

- In Ezekiel 39, we hear again of Israel's restoration. The Lord says the people will forget their shame and return to dwell in their own land.

- Similarly, while on earth, we are living "in exile" from our true home—heaven.

- As we have seen, everything that the Lord allows to happen to his people—whether it be destruction, exile, or restoration—is to help them know who he is and to bring them back to him.

Take It to **Prayer**

Father in heaven, we give you praise and glory. We ask that you please watch over our hearts and our minds. Watch over what we say, the words we speak. Watch over the thoughts of our minds, and the desires of our hearts, Lord God. Because we know that we are good. We are made in your image and likeness. But we are also fallen. We are good but broken, good but fallen. And so we know that our minds are meant to know truth and our hearts are meant to love the true and the good and the beautiful. Our hearts are meant to love you. And our mouths have been given to us to speak truth and to never deceive, to never blaspheme, but only to build up, never to tear down. And so, Lord God, we ask you to please touch our minds with your Spirit so we can be filled with your truth and understand truthfully. Touch our hearts with your Spirit that we can love as you love. And touch our mouths, Lord God, that we don't pour out folly but we only say the words that people really need to hear, words that will help them. Maybe words that will help them, but also not only words to build up the people around us but also words that glorify the Lord. In Jesus' name we pray. Amen.

Dive **Deeper**

Today, ask the Lord's blessing, that you may find
joy and peace in knowing him.

Reflect on the **Word**

- Jeremiah 10 speaks of how idolatry has brought ruin on Israel. Those who worship idols become like the idols themselves—foolish and stupid.

- When we give our hearts and minds over to anything other than God, we become foolish. When we give our hearts to something, we give our minds to it as well.

- As we have seen, there is a twofold movement of repentance—distrust of self and trust in the Lord. This is what Jeremiah is saying here—the people need to trust in the Lord, not in anything else.

- In Jeremiah 11, we see the prophet preaching against Israel and Judah for violating the covenant.

- Some are plotting against Jeremiah for his words. They try to kill him by throwing him in a cistern.

- In the end, Jeremiah is taken with some of the people of Jerusalem to Egypt, where he will die in exile.

- At first glance, it seems that Jeremiah dies a complete and utter failure. He preaches for nearly fifty years and no one seems to listen. Like Jesus, he speaks the truth and is hated for it.

- Saints of the Church have seen Ezekiel's visions through a New Testament lens. There is a spiritual interpretation of Ezekiel's vision of the Temple. For example, St. Gregory the Great in a homily says that the Temple entrances of Ezekiel 40 represent a gate for sinners coming from a place of coldness (the north); a gate for warm, virtuous souls (the south); and a gate for those who are on a path of penitence (the east).[*]

---

[*] Gregory the Great, *Homilies on Ezekiel* 2.7.13, in *Ancient Christian Commentary on Scripture: Old Testament*, ed. Thomas C. Oden, vol. 13, *Ezekiel, Daniel*, ed. Kenneth Stevenson and Michael Glerup (Downers Grove, IL: InterVarsity Press, 2008), 134, books.google.com.

Take It to **Prayer**

Father in heaven, we give you praise and glory. Thank you so much. Thank you once again for bringing us back to this day, this new day that you've given to us, a day where we can receive your Word, a day that we get to ... even if we struggled through, Lord, thank you so much. You continue to speak to us. You continue to call us to yourself. And you continue to call us to repentance. Even in the midst of confusion. Even in the midst of your Word that we don't necessarily understand. And especially in the midst of your Word that we don't respond to with genuine hearts, with authentic hearts, and with truly repentant hearts. Help us to repent. Help us to turn back to you more and more every single day so that you may be glorified and your people may be sanctified. We ask this in the name of Jesus Christ, our Lord. Amen.

Dive **Deeper**

OLIVE TREE IN GETHSEMANE

Through the prophet Jeremiah, God warns that Israel, once a fruitful olive tree, is now in danger of being burned up and consumed for its disobedience and idolatry. (See Jeremiah 11.)

Reflect on the **Word**

- Proverbs 15:9-12 touches on the virtue of docility, which is the ability to be taught. A person with a docile heart is open to whatever God wishes to teach him or her.

- In Jeremiah 12:5, we are asked, "If you have raced with men on foot, and they have wearied you, how will you compete with horses?" In other words, if we cannot compete with certain people, why should we expect to compete with the workings of God? It is wise to acknowledge our limitations.

- As always, Jeremiah calls the people to repentance. He is also telling them to brace for the impact of the destruction that is coming. Jeremiah 12, though, ends with a message of hope from the Lord.

- In Jeremiah 13, we see the image of the linen waistcloth (or underwear). The Lord tells Jeremiah to buy a new linen waistcloth and wear it, then hide it near the Euphrates, where it will rot away. This is a metaphor for God's people.

- At the conclusion of Jeremiah 13, we hear a call to come back to the Lord while there is still time. These words are applicable to us as well.

Take It to **Prayer**

Father in heaven, we give you praise and glory. We thank you so much. Thank you, Lord, for the gift of your Word. Thank you for the gift of just being able to be a part of this community, to know that there are people praying for us and with us, people who are listening to your Word—all of us who are broken, all of us who struggle with so many things, and yet we continue to come back to this place. We continue to allow you to speak to us. We continue to give you permission to know our hearts, and you do. And you do speak to us. And you do know our hearts, Lord God. Even in the midst of our woundedness, even in the midst of our brokenness, even in the midst of how we have failed to be the kind of men and women that you have created and redeemed us to be, you still call us back to yourself. Thank you so much. And may you be glorified. May you be praised. May you be loved not only by the hearts around this world, but also by our hearts. May our hearts be the kinds of hearts that can love you the way you deserve to be loved. In Jesus' name we pray. Amen.

Dive **Deeper**

In your prayer time today, meditate on the virtue of docility. Consider whether your heart is docile, ready to accept whatever the Lord wants to teach you.

Reflect on the **Word**

- In Proverbs 15, we see that if we are poor materially but have reverence for God, we are better off than those who have great wealth but are troubled.

- In Jeremiah 14, we hear of the nobles who send their servants for water, but the cisterns are dry and they return with none. Similarly, when we have been unfaithful to the Lord, we can find ourselves dry.

- In Jeremiah 14:13, we again hear of the false prophets who are preaching lies to the people. There are false prophets in our day, those who speak compelling or consoling words that can lead us away from God.

- In Jeremiah 14, the prophet does not water down his message—instead, he speaks of destruction and devastation. He allows the truth of his words to break his heart.

- Ezekiel's vision of the glory of the Lord coming back to the rebuilt Temple contrasts with his earlier vision of the Lord's glory departing from it due to the people's idolatry.

- Sometimes, the Spirit of the Lord can depart, and we might not even realize it at first—as we saw with Samson after Delilah cut his hair (see Judges 16:20).

- Jesus gives us the Holy Spirit. We need to always walk, speak, and love with the power and presence of the Spirit rather than relying on our own strength.

Take It to **Prayer**

Father in heaven, we give you praise and thank you so much. God, please receive our praise today. Please receive our voice. Receive our heart. Receive, God, our gift of thanksgiving. Because this day, none of us did anything to deserve it. It's just your gift to us. And so we give it back to you. We give it back to you in praise. We give it back to you in thanksgiving. And we give it back to you with humble hearts. Because, Lord God, we did nothing to deserve it. So may you be praised this day and every day in Jesus' name. Amen.

Engraving by F. van Bleyswyck in
Calmet's Dictionary of the Bible

Dive **Deeper**

TEMPLE ALTAR

This image shows an artist's rendition of the altar in the Temple of Solomon (bottom) and the altar as described by the prophet in Ezekiel 43 (top).

Reflect on the **Word**

- Proverbs 15:17 reminds us that there are things in this world that are more important than material goods—family, love, peace, joy, and knowing the Lord.

- In Proverbs 15:20, we are told that a child's decision to pursue the path of wisdom or foolishness can bring either joy or sorrow to his parents. As the old saying goes, parents are only as happy as their least happy child.

- In Jeremiah 16, the Lord tells the prophet that he is not to have a wife or children.

- In this chapter, we again hear that the Lord will bring his people back to their own land.

- Jeremiah 17 refers to the sin of Judah—which is trusting in anything other than the Lord. The person who trusts in the Lord is compared to a tree that does not need to worry about water or nutrients because it is planted in the right place.

- In Jeremiah, God makes it clear that his people must observe the Sabbath rest—and, when they do so, the Messiah will come. This provides the context for why the Pharisees were so upset when Jesus cured on the Sabbath.

- In Ezekiel, we hear that those who enter the Temple through the north gate will exit through the south, and those who enter through the south gate will exit through the north. When one enters into the Lord's presence and worships him, he cannot leave the same way he came. This should be the same with us at Mass—we should leave transformed.

Take It to **Prayer**

Father in heaven, we give you praise and glory. Thank you so much for this opportunity. Thank you for bringing us to day 236. What a gift that you are. And what a gift each day, Lord, this entire time, every one of these days … none of them are days that we deserve. Every one of them is a day that you have given to us as a free gift. And all you ask is that we simply receive it. All you ask is that we receive it with gratitude and thanksgiving knowing that none of these days is anything that any of us have ever deserved. And so you simply ask us to receive it. And then on top of receiving it, to use it just for your glory. To say yes to you. To say yes to your gift. And to receive this gift that you may be glorified. And to use this gift that your children might be helped, loved, and cared for. And so please, Lord God, help us to receive this day as your gift—days of difficulty and days of blessing—but also help us to use this day. Help us to use this difficulty that comes with today so that those around us who are carrying heavy burdens might carry a little bit lighter burdens because of us. Help us to glorify you. Help us to lift up our brothers and sisters. Help us to let you love us. And help us to love you in return. In Jesus' name we pray. Amen.

Dive **Deeper**

In prayer today, consider the way you view the Mass.
Ask the Lord for the grace to be transformed by being
in his presence and worshipping him at Mass.

Reflect on the **Word**

- Jeremiah 18 begins by comparing Israel to potter's clay, which can be reworked by the potter into any vessel he chooses. In this analogy, God is the potter. Regardless of our past, God can shape us into the future he wills for us.

- In Jeremiah 18, we also hear of plotting against Jeremiah by those who have trusted in the falsehoods they have heard from their leaders and false prophets. They have been telling the people what they want to hear.

- At the end of Jeremiah 18, the prophet is angry with the people for plotting against him. Similarly, Moses became angry when he led Israel during the Exodus.

- God tells Jeremiah in chapter 19 to buy a potter's flask and take some of the elders with him to the valley of Hinnom where children have been sacrificed. There, he will shatter the potter's flask as an image of what will happen to the people when Babylon conquers them.

- Jeremiah does not revel in his prophecy of coming destruction. This is simply a consequence of the people's actions.

- Like the people of Jeremiah's time, our actions have consequences. We must repent and seek God's forgiveness while we have time.

- At the conclusion of Ezekiel, we have the image of water running from underneath the right side of the Temple to the east. This living water will bring life to the sea. This is a prophecy of how the Lord will not only bring his people back from Babylon but ultimately bring life to the entire world in Jesus.

- On every crucifix, there is the mark of the spear on the side of Jesus' body. From John's Gospel, we know that a Roman soldier pierced his side with a lance and blood and water flowed out (see John 19:34). The Fathers of the Church saw this as a symbol of Baptism and the Eucharist. Here, we see the connection between Jesus's body and the Temple.

Take It to **Prayer**

Father in heaven, we give you praise. Thank you so much. Thank you so much for this day. And thank you so much for bringing us back to your Word on this day. You are a gift. Your Word is a gift. This day, Lord God, whatever day this is in our lives, it is day 237 of just listening to your Word. And we thank you so much for continuing to speak to us, not only speaking to our minds and revealing you to us, but also speaking to our hearts and moving our hearts to belong to you with everything we have and with everything we are. We thank you. We give you praise. And we bless your name. In Jesus' name we pray. Amen.

Dive **Deeper**

Look at a crucifix and notice the mark of the spear in Jesus' side. Praise God for his mercy and love. Reflect on how he desires to mold you, like a potter, into someone resembling himself, regardless of your sins and your past.

Reflect on the **Word**

- In Jeremiah 20, the prophet is put in the stocks. We sense how hurt he is by this unjust treatment. He says, "O Lᴏʀᴅ, you have deceived me" (Jeremiah 20:7).

- While Jeremiah faithfully speaks the Lord's truth, he is surrounded by false prophets who have no problem with lying. They falsely proclaim that God will deliver his people from Babylon.

- Jeremiah, in chapter 21, reiterates that the Lord will allow Jerusalem to fall. We hear Jeremiah's distress at this message in language similar to that of Job.

- The book of Daniel contains familiar stories and also recounts revelations. Daniel and Jeremiah are contemporaries.

- In Babylon, Daniel and three companions are trained for three years in the king's house. They refuse to eat from the king's table but instead eat only food permissible according to the Law. The Lord blesses them for being faithful.

- This story shows us that faithfulness to God can still be practiced even in the midst of exile. We see how the people of God should live when they are not in their own land.

- In Daniel 2, we have the story of Nebuchadnezzar's dream. He wants it interpreted, but he requires the interpreter to share not only its meaning but the dream itself. When Daniel is called on by the king to interpret his dream, he asks Hananiah, Azariah, and Mishael to pray with him. When he correctly recounts and interprets Nebuchadnezzar's dream, he gives all credit to the Lord rather than to his own wisdom.

- Nebuchadnezzar's dream is of a statue made of different materials, representing Babylon, Persia, Greece, Rome, and the kingdom God establishes—the Church.

Take It to **Prayer**

Father in heaven, we thank you so much. We give you praise and glory. Lord God, thank you so much not only for your wisdom in Proverbs, but also for helping us follow along with Jeremiah, the weeping prophet, and thank you for introducing us to Daniel and his companions, Hananiah, Azariah, and Mishael. We thank you so much for the gift that you are, the gift that these prophets have been to us, to the world, to history, and how they just keep pointing back to you, keep pointing to your truth. Help us to walk in your truth and live in your truth this day and every day of our lives. In Jesus' name we pray. Amen.

Dive **Deeper**

What is the meaning *of the statue in Nebuchadnezzar's dream?*

In Daniel 2:31-35, Daniel recounts to Nebuchadnezzar what he saw in his dream: a statue of different materials. Daniel's interpretation of this image describes four successive world powers, followed by a fifth kingdom that will topple them all. The head of gold is Babylon; the breast and arms of silver are Persia; the belly and thighs of bronze are Greece; and the legs of iron are Rome. It seems that the feet of iron and clay are not a kingdom but the political fragmentation in the last days.

Daniel 2:44 concludes that God will establish an everlasting kingdom. This fifth kingdom is described as a stone "cut out by no human hand" that broke the statue to dust and "became a great mountain and filled the whole earth" (Daniel 2:34-35). This refers to the kingdom of God, which was established by the coming of Jesus—the Church.

–Jeff Cavins

Reflect on the **Word**

- In Jeremiah 22, the prophet calls the king of Judah to repentance.

- The people of the covenant are called to be faithful to the Lord—and to take care of the poor, orphans, widows, and strangers. The Lord's people must care for those who have no one to care for them.

- In Babylon, the names of Daniel, Hananiah, Azariah, and Mishael are changed to refer to false gods of Babylon. Yet they refuse to behave like the Babylonians.

- In Daniel 3, King Nebuchadnezzar erects a golden statue but learns that Hananiah, Azariah, and Mishael will not bow to it. He warns them that if they do not, he will throw them into a furnace.

- They respond to the king's threats by saying that the Lord can deliver them, but even if he will not, they still will not bow down to the statue.

- The three men survive, and Nebuchadnezzar then declares that anyone who insults the God of Hananiah, Azariah, and Mishael will be put to death.

Take It to **Prayer**

Father in heaven, we thank you so much. We give you praise and glory. Thank you so much for your Word. Thank you for speaking to us and for constantly reaching out and constantly revealing your heart to us. We ask that you please help our hearts to receive you, and help our hearts to hear you, and help our hearts to be more like you. Help us to love what you love—in doing so, to be your image in this world so that those that see us ... they get a glimpse at you. We make this prayer in the name of Jesus Christ, our Lord. Amen.

Dive **Deeper**

RUINS OF BABYLON

This image depicts the ruins of the ancient city of Babylon (in modern-day Iraq). Jeremiah and Daniel both speak of this city and its king, Nebuchadnezzar.

Reflect on the **Word**

- Proverbs 16:3 reminds us that everything we do we should do for God.

- In Jeremiah 23:23, we are reminded that God is near; he is not just watching us from some distant place.

- According to the second commandment, we must not take the name of the Lord in vain. We should never use God's name carelessly, and we should never do anything in the Lord's name that he does not want us to do.

- Daniel 4 shows how Nebuchadnezzar, king of Babylon, is humbled before the Lord. His power, majesty, and reason are removed so that he can see that the Lord is the true God.

- In Daniel 5, we hear the story of Belshazzar and the handwriting on the wall, which tells him he will be succeeded by the Persians. Here, we have the transition of power from Babylon to Persia.

- While we can easily become preoccupied with what is happening in the world, politics, or culture, we need to remember that nations rise and fall, people come and go—but the Lord remains forever. We are called to humble ourselves before God, seeking to love and serve him in all things and to love our neighbor as ourselves.

Take It to **Prayer**

*Father in heaven, we give you praise and glory. We thank you so much. Thank you
for this day. Thank you for a new day. Thank you for bringing us to this moment
where we get to not only hear your Word, but we get to be united. We get to be
united as a group of people, as a community of people, who are listening to your
Word and are bound together not only by your love for us, our love for you, your
Word, and also this bond of prayer—that we lift each other up in prayer every
single day because we need your grace, and we need each other. We cannot
make this journey on our own. You have not left us orphans. You have called us
your sons and daughters. You have become our Father. You made us brothers and
sisters from all across the world, Lord God. From every race, from every ethnicity,
from every nationality, we are united by your Holy Spirit, and we are truly brothers
and sisters belonging to you, our true Dad, our true Father. Thank you.
Please hear our prayer in Jesus' name. Amen.*

Dive **Deeper**

ENGRAVING
OF KING
NEBUCHADNEZZAR

*The Babylonian ziggurat
shown here was dedicated to
a false deity honored in
Nebuchadnezzar's time.*

Reflect on the **Word**

- In Jeremiah 24, we hear about Zedekiah, under whom the final wave of deportations to Babylon takes place.

- In Jeremiah 24, the prophet is shown two baskets of figs—one good, the other bad. The good figs represent those who have already been exiled, while the bad figs represent those who have stayed in Jerusalem or gone to Egypt.

- Jeremiah is among those who go to Egypt, as he will remain with God's people. He will remain among those who are "bad figs."

- In exile in Babylon, the people of God will have their hearts set right. The Lord uses King Nebuchadnezzar to accomplish this—even though he enslaves and kills many. God sometimes permits evil to accomplish his will.

- Finally, when the Lord's people return to their land after the Exile, idolatry ceases.

- In Daniel 6, we again see the Israelites' refusal to conform to the people around them.

- Today, we hear the familiar story of Daniel in the lions' den. Even if we are faithful to the Lord, people can still conspire against us. Yet the Lord will save us if we trust in him.

- Daniel, Hananiah, Azariah, and Mishael offer a powerful example of how to live in exile. As Christians, we too are in exile—this is not our ultimate home.

- In Daniel 7, we have a description of the prophet's vision of four beasts representing different kingdoms: Babylon, the Medo-Persian Empire, Greece, and Rome. Daniel also sees the Ancient of Days and "one like a son of man" coming with the clouds (Daniel 7:13).

- Though we live in unstable times, we know that God, the Ancient of Days, conquers all—and has invited us to be part of his kingdom.

Take It to **Prayer**

Father in heaven, we give you praise and glory. We thank you so much for reminding us of your truth and for reminding us of the pieces of wisdom that we need to never, ever forget. Help us to always remember not only the wisdom we need to make it through this life, but also help us to always remember what you have done in our lives, what you have done in the lives of your people, and what you have done in this world. Lord God, help us to belong to you more than we belong to anything else. Help us to be yours more than we are anything else. We ask this in the name of Jesus Christ, our Lord. Amen.

Dive **Deeper**

Who are the satraps *mentioned in the book of Daniel?*

In the book of Daniel, we see mention of *satraps*. But who were they?

In the Babylonian empire, there were several classes of officials who helped the king rule. Satraps were among these, serving in a powerful position as they maintained order within the empire. The book of Daniel also mentions justices, treasurers, and governors, among others (see Daniel 3:2).

As we see in Daniel 3, the three young Jewish officials of the king named Shadrach, Meshach, and Abednego would not worship the king's idol of gold along with the other officials, and so they were cast into the fiery furnace.

–Jeff Cavins

Reflect on the **Word**

- Jeremiah 26 takes us back to the beginning of the reign of Jehoiakim, son of Josiah.

- As we have seen, Jeremiah begins his prophetic mission under Josiah, a mission which continues under Jehoiakim. After Jehoiakim, we jump forward to the reign of Zedekiah, the final king under whom Jeremiah preaches.

- Jeremiah is frequently threatened with death because he speaks the truth. We see this in Jeremiah 26 when the priests and false prophets condemn him. Rather than killing him, though, the princes and the people acknowledge his message. Here, Jeremiah is compared to the prophet Micah, whose call to repentance at the time of Hezekiah was heeded.

- In Jeremiah 27, we read that Zedekiah, the final king of Judah before the last deportation, begins his reign. When Nebuchadnezzar comes to Jerusalem, he kills Zedekiah's sons in front of him and then gouges out Zedekiah's eyes before sending him into exile (see 2 Kings 25:7).

- In Daniel 8, we have the vision of a ram and a goat—the ram with the two horns representing Media and Persia, and the goat representing the nation of Greece.

- Prophecy is frequently shrouded in symbolic imagery to convey a deeper meaning.

- The Lord gives a timeline of seventy weeks of years (or nearly five hundred years) until the coming of the Anointed One.

Take It to **Prayer**

Father in heaven, we give you praise and glory. We thank you so much. It is true that we plan our own ways, but you direct our steps. And when we belong to you, when we're open to you, when we listen to you, when we obey your Word, even when we are simply humble, Lord, there is almost nothing that can replace just a humility before your voice, a humility before your will and before your Word. Yes, we plan our ways. But you direct our steps, Lord God. Help us to continually follow you, to be guided and shaped by your Word, and for every step we take to be done in faith. For every step we take to be done in hope. And every step we take to be done out of love for you and for our neighbor. For you are love. And you call us to love you and to receive your love, to love our neighbor and to be your love for them. Help us to do this. Help us to be this. In Jesus' name we pray. Amen.

Dive **Deeper**

***What is Daniel** talking about when he mentions saints?*

Certain people in the Old Testament are revered as saints in the New Covenant, even though they never received the Baptism of the New Covenant.

Daniel prophesies about the coming of the Messiah, Jesus, whom he refers to as the "son of man"—the one who will be "given dominion and glory and kingdom, that all peoples, nations, and languages should serve him" (Daniel 7:13-14). His kingdom will be everlasting.

This everlasting kingdom is the Church. In Daniel's vision, the saints suffer under the persecution of the fourth kingdom that makes war with the saints. In the end, the saints, as part of the kingdom of the Messiah, the Church, will reign along with Jesus. As the angel interprets for Daniel, "Their kingdom shall be an everlasting kingdom, and all dominions shall serve and obey them" (Daniel 7:27).

–Kara Logan

Reflect on the **Word**

- In Jeremiah 28, we see Hananiah, the false prophet, proclaiming that in two years Nebuchadnezzar is going to fall and that the people of Israel will return. In Jeremiah 28:10, we are told that Hananiah takes the yoke off of Jeremiah's neck and breaks it, causing Jeremiah to prophesy that it will be replaced with a yoke of iron.

- Since the people will not repent or accept that they are going to be destroyed, the wooden yoke that is mercy will be replaced by an iron yoke of punishment.

- We can sometimes look at the commandments of God as a yoke or burden, but they are a wooden yoke. If we do not submit to that yoke, God often allows us to experience the consequences—the iron yoke of punishment.

- Hananiah dies within two months, having been rebuked for his false prophesies.

- In Jeremiah 29, we see the prophet's letters to the people in Babylon telling them how to live in exile. He tells them that they will be there for seventy years. They should go ahead and build lives in exile but always remember that they will be returning home.

- In this chapter, we also have the promise that God has not abandoned his people; he has a future in store for them. God always has a plan for our lives.

- In Daniel 10, the prophet has a vision of an angel, who appears to him after he has been doing penance. The angel tells Daniel that God heard his prayers from the moment he began to pray but there is more going on in the divine plan.

- Daniel's prophecy in chapter 11 is fulfilled. (As a result, some who do not believe in biblical prophecy believe that Daniel 11 was written after the fact.) The prophecy speaks of the coming of Alexander the Great, who, since he dies without an heir, is succeeded by four of his generals.

- We are told that "the people who know their God shall stand firm and take action" (Daniel 11:32). Even amid the devastation that is coming, God is fighting for his people.

Take It to **Prayer**

Father in heaven, we give you praise and give you glory. We thank you so much.
Thank you so much for this day. Thank you so much for your Word poured out for
us, your Word given to our hearts, and your Word declared to us. We ask that you
help us understand it and help us apply it to our lives this day and every day.
We pray in the name of Jesus Christ, our Lord. Amen.

Dive **Deeper**

A YOKE

This image shows a yoke, which was put around the necks of oxen to
enable them to pull a plow. Jeremiah 28 employs the language of a yoke
several times to describe God's plan.

Our Story continues in Volume III ...

APPENDIX

How Do We Speak the Truth When It Is Difficult?

Because of our Baptism, all of us are called to be prophets and to speak the truth. Here are some ways to speak when it is difficult.

- Pray to the Holy Spirit before talking to your family members and friends. Pray for the grace that you may speak the words that they need to hear in a way that moves their hearts. Ask the Holy Spirit to prepare their hearts to receive the truth.

- Pray for boldness to tell the truth without fear and not just say what people want to hear.

- Seek to develop a relationship with anti-Catholic friends and family members so that they may know that you love them and want what is best for them. Then they will be more open to hearing what you have to say.

- Remember that you are merely an instrument of the Lord. You cannot move a person's heart to repentance; only the Holy Spirit can. Do not take it personally when others do not listen to you or when they reject you. If you receive persecution in speaking the truth, rejoice and take comfort in the fact that you have done what the Lord is asking of you.

- Remember your call. The Lord will ask you to account for the words you have said, as well as for those you did not say— but should have (see Matthew 12:36).

-Kara Logan